Are you ready to listen? —God

Tapping into Divinely Guided Healing and Self Love

VOLUME 1

DEBBIE N. GOLDBERG

SMOAKHOUSE PUBLISHING

Copyright © 2016 by Debbie N. Goldberg

All rights reserved. No part of this publication may be reproduced, distributed, or transmitted in any form or by any means, including photocopying, recording, or other electronic or mechanical methods, without the prior written permission of the publisher, except in the case of brief quotations embodied in critical reviews and certain other noncommercial uses permitted by copyright law. For permission requests, write to the publisher, addressed "Attention: Permissions Coordinator," at the address below.

Smoakhouse Publishing
1313 Mockingbird Rd
Key Largo, FL 33037
www.smoakhousebooks.com

Ordering Information:
Quantity sales. Special discounts are available on quantity purchases by corporations, associations, and others. For details, contact the publisher at the address above.

Printed in the United States of America

Library of Congress Cataloging-in-Publication Data
2016962445

Goldberg, Debbie N.
Are you ready to listen? – God : Tapping into Divinely Guided Healing and Self-Love / Debbie N. Goldberg
ISBN 978-0-9983227-0-4
1. Self-Help : Religion & Spirituality 2. New Age & Spirituality : Mental & Spiritual Healing 3. Practices & Sacred Texts : Unitarian Universalism

Book design by Elena Reznikova

Second Edition

♡ The Warrior of Love

Will you rise up with me today in quest of healing and love so that the earth can rise and expand with love? It is something that each one of us needs to do no matter what type of method we use to open our heart to hope and humanity and to find the blessings within and without. There needs to be a concerted persistent effort on everyone's part to relieve themselves of the pain and suffering that resides within them and to help those who, at present, are unable to do this work. As we clear ourselves of our pain and suffering we are shifting others' energy in ways that create a positive ripple effect across the entire planet. We have that much power and do not know it. I know this seems a lot to take in but it is the truth. It is the only truth. The more you love yourself you have a positive effect on the whole planet, since we are all a single, collective consciousness; we are one. This work is hard but it needs to be done. As you do this work you are set free from the chains of suffering and now have freedom to be happy and create the life and world you want. The Creator lives in each one of us, the God within, the Warrior of Love. Open your heart and allow love to reign in your life so others can learn to do the same just by feeling your love. Bless this day as the start of your journey inward to transmute and transform everything into love.

Shalom.

♡

To my children, their families, grandchildren and the ones yet to come. For if I have done my job of healing myself and come into who I truly am then I have paved the way for you and contributed to your own spiritual path of love, healing and purpose—there is no greater gift that parents can give their children. As I heal from generational transmissions of family pain and my own experiences it automatically sets you up to do the same. It is a gift of love from the bottom of my heart. I hold you all in such high esteem, love, and light for you have been my greatest teachers. These books are my legacy of love to you.

♡

To you—this book is a gift of profound love from Jesus. Through me, Jesus delivers a message to you that must be heard in order for you to live a life of happiness, gratitude, love, healing and purpose.

Contents

Preface xi

Background 3

    Chapter 1: *Meeting God* 7

    Chapter 2: *A Spiritual Framework to Understand Your Life* 11

    Chapter 3: *Keep Going Inside* 19

    Chapter 4: *Let This Book Re-Parent You Spiritually* 25

    Chapter 5: *The Kingdom of Heaven is Within Us and Always Has Been* 33

    Chapter 6: *The Blessings of Programing* 41

    Chapter 7: *What Is It We Truly Want? What's Missing?* 45

    Chapter 8: *Life in the Fast Lane* 49

    Chapter 9: *Where Does All the Sickness Come From Anyway?* 53

    Chapter 10: *Beginning to See Your Truth* 59

    Chapter 11: *Faith versus Trust* 65

    Chapter 12: *Mind Blowing* 71

    Chapter 13: *We Are All Self-Sufficient* 75

    Chapter 14: *This Energy Will Follow You* 79

    Chapter 15: *It's Crunch Time* 83

    Chapter 16: *So What Does All of This Mean?* 89

    Chapter 17: *Consciously Creating* 93

About the Author 99

Acknowledgements 101

Preface

This is my story, my journey to healing and a more spiritually driven life. This is my dance between my ego/shadow side and my soul, the pervasive rhythm of the highs and lows, like the waves that caress the shore. It is the pulse of life. It is the same as our breath and all motion.

I humbly come before you with these words knowing that I have had no formal training in spirituality, physics, science or theology. The beautiful divine wisdom offered in these books has come to me through my spiritual guidance, Jesus, who has graced me with the task of passing these teachings on to you.

I was given the task of writing these words and I have done so to the best of my ability. My understanding and interpretation of what was passed along (channeled) through me is imperfect since it comes through the filter of my own ego/programming and yet it is perfect as my spirit knows it to be true. All of the words, blessings and poetry have come through me, not from me, except where I give examples of my own experiences and discuss methods of other teachers that I've used in working with my clients and in healing myself. I don't claim to have proof of what I say or to have personally integrated all the wisdom written here. The process discussed in this series of books represents a life's journey if not many lives. As I evolve through this life and become evermore ready to receive, I trust that I will be able to more fully understand and internalize the wisdom presented here.

Over the centuries, both scholars and non-scholars have presented interpretations of Jesus' teachings. Others have channeled messages from Jesus in order to clarify his teachings. The time has come for a simpler explanation of why we are here and what it is we are to do in order to fully enjoy this life we have been given. Although the concepts may be difficult, they are not new.

Life is complicated. Our struggle to gain knowledge and wisdom is never ending. The information contained in these books is truth through Jesus. The information contained herein is not complete in and of itself; there is so much more. These books are meant to help you get started on a spiritual journey so you can find and follow your own divine path.

Are you ready to listen?

—God

Background

I am a 58-year old white, married, Jewish female born in Brooklyn, NY. I am what you would call a cultural Jew, not having been raised religious but having always been spiritual and believing in God since a young child but not knowing how or why.

I came from a hard working middle-class family. My early life was filled with suffering and grief. I experienced emotional, physical and sexual abuse. I have been married twice and have two beautiful children from my first marriage (I am forever grateful Don) and am now a grandma with our family continually growing.

I have worked hard all of my life. I've been a secretary, bookkeeper, jewelry storeowner, waitress, bartender, and student. In my 30's, I experienced a spiritual awakening in the form of an intense dream that laid-out my career plans. I knew it was a divinely orchestrated message from God. That dream sent me off to college for the first time to study therapy/counseling. I followed my dream and never looked back.

I now know that I was led to practice counseling so that I could heal myself. For several years I had a thriving clinical private practice but then started to wonder: 'Is this it? Is this what I will be doing the rest of my life?' I felt happy and enjoyed my life at the time but I began to question whether I was fulfilled even though I loved working with my clients, my business partner and coworkers, external support staff (thank you all for believing in me, holding me up and being angels in my life). We were a loving work family. It was a very comfortable existence.

After a family conflict in June of 2014, I started looking deeper into myself. I was led to Dr. Margaret Paul and attended a weekend workshop in September 2014; it was a divine blessing. What I learned is that although I thought I had healed myself from painful events in my life, I had not. I was living unconsciously (not present), asleep at the wheel of life, even though I thought I had experienced my spiritual awakening 25 years earlier.

I had been suppressing and repressing my feelings and had been living my life through my ego, its fears and irrational programing. I was living my life based on my own personal egocentric story of who I thought I was, who I thought everyone else was, and how I fit into the world.

I realize now that I had never learned that I was responsible for my own feelings, thoughts, behaviors, self-worth and lovability. Like everyone else, I was looking for myself outside of myself. I knew there was always something guiding me, God, Spirit, a force, the universe; I didn't know what to call it. It wasn't until I started to work on myself spiritually and finally came to know my spiritual guidance, Jesus, on an intimate level that I understood the divinity with which we are all graced.

A specific meditation taught me that I can see, hear, and converse with the spiritual realm which I will discuss more in the following pages. I have kept a journal of almost all of my conversations with the spiritual realm since. That revelation has changed my life profoundly, and for that I am forever grateful. All the love I had been searching for on the outside was inside the whole time. I have since come to know a much more personal relationship with God and now realize that we all have many other guides such as angels and those that have passed on before us. I struggle to express the depth and breadth of the love that was revealed to me since I cannot find the words to describe it. This love resides inside of each one of us.

BACKGROUND

My life's journey is to master my inner-world and stop trying to master the outer world, to cultivate the art of love within myself. As I continue on my journey I stumble at times, take steps backwards, move forward, and then backward again. I am just like you.

I am thankful for being spiritually led back to Dr. Barbara De Angelis in October 2015 for a "Soul Shifts" workshop and for her guidance in helping me as I continue my work to understand my spiritual path and myself.

As I move forward, I have come to understand that all truth and all of the answers we need are already inside us. We need to direct our questions inward. No one taught us how to do this in school or at home. It is helpful to have guides and spiritual mentors who are available to you, to help you navigate and reassure you as you begin your inward journey. As humans, we are always seeking reassurance, especially when we delve into a world of unknowns, our inner world, and the spiritual world within. The truth is, everything you need to know is within.

These books outline what I have learned on my own personal journey to date. I know there will be much more to learn as I co-create my life with God and journey along my path.

My hope is to take everything I have learned and with which I have been graced to inspire you to heal and move toward your own spiritual journey and learn the art of love.

I pray blessings that these books bring you to a place of co-creation of your life's purpose. God—Please bestow the blessings you have bestowed upon me to the readers of these books; heal me and heal them.

Awakening from the sleep/unconsciousness, healing, and following my personal spiritual journey is the hardest, most rewarding and most fulfilling work I have ever done. Don't be afraid. The work you are about to do is a gift of love to yourself and becomes much easier as you paddle down the river of life with guidance, love, passion and purpose.

We each have a Spiritual Master within as well as many Spiritual Guides. We never go through our Spiritual Awakening alone, even though at times it may seem as if we have no one to guide us. By going inside yourself and earnestly seeking your Spiritual Master you will discover your own special course of spiritual instruction. It is designed just for you.

Your soul is already anchored, grounded, and rooted in God and this journey. Your soul chose the life path you are traveling. This is why we need to look within for guidance before relying on just outside sources and remedies.

I too have repeatedly fallen victim to forgetting that everything I need is within me. I have often been hijacked by my ego looking to external sources for guidance. In such times we have to find the strength to return to our base, our spiritual foundation. Our true answers will always be found within.

Chapter One

Meeting God

*There is no greater gift than to
Awaken and hear the voice of God*

It was November 13, 2014. I stayed home from work with laryngitis that had been lingering for weeks. I realized I needed to rest my voice. In retrospect, I think I needed to get to a point where I could no longer speak; I could just listen. I believe my soul brought me to that place, as uncomfortable as it was. I had already been speaking with and seeing Jesus for the past two months and knew there was more to see and learn. It was a good time to catch up on my spiritual work so I created a little office space on my bed and started to work on Margaret Paul's 30-day online 'Raise Your Vibration' course and at the same time Derek Rydall's 'Soul Purpose Blueprint.'

This is the story of my life, multitasking, pushing myself even through sickness with little regard for how it affects me. For two days I had been in deep meditation and prayer as I was working these two programs. Completely surrendered to God, I was begging for help in understanding my life's purpose. All of a sudden I heard an inner voice, a male voice saying: "Are you ready to listen?" I knew it was God's voice, however, I had no idea what was coming next. I was a little scared at first but then I thought about what he said and I started to laugh.

I understood what God meant because throughout my life I never really listened to anyone or anything. At some point as a young child, I had simply shut down. My loud and abusive father (who I have now totally forgiven and have great love for him) was constantly telling me that I was a bad girl. Constantly it was: "You never listen" or "You need to listen to me." His words and hands were harsh and the anxiety it created in me was so fierce that the only way I could cope and resist being controlled was to close my ears. I understand this now but did not recognize this throughout most of my life.

As I smiled, I perked up and said, "Yes, God, I am ready to listen!" He told me that I needed to write down everything that I hear and that I needed to listen to my heart. All of a sudden I heard a line from one of my favorite songs: "Take it all, take it all, put my life in your hands." It brought me to tears of joy and deeper surrender.

Then I heard an inner voice singing to me: "Can you hear me? I am a miracle and so are you. You are a beautiful sweet little miracle and how I love you. I am everywhere with you and love you truly." I then hear God's voice again saying, "She needs you to love her; she is in your heart." I instantly knew that God was referring to my inner child. At that moment, I saw a vision of a beautiful little girl with brown hair wrapped in my green prayer shawl. As a child, I found my security from a satin-lined blanket. I wondered now if my prayer shawl was offering me security inside this vision. I heard God's voice again saying, "She is born in my heart and you are the sweetest little girl in my heart."

At this point, my ego kicks in and says to God in a sarcastic tone, "I bet you say that to all the girls." As soon as I heard what came out of my mouth I was ashamed and appalled and immediately begged for forgiveness.

Of course, God forgave me and had me listen to my inner child who then dictated a beautiful story about a little girl and how she learned about God. It was enchanting and I was completely overwhelmed by what I was hearing and learning and by the love that was coming through me. My ego couldn't stand it and angrily said to God, "So this is it? This is my purpose in life? This is the big thing I am to do? This is what I am working so hard for, this little children's story?"

Again, I couldn't believe the dismissiveness and disregard that ran out of my mouth. I threw myself on the floor and begged forgiveness again that I could even think such a thing. I cried and cried with regret. I realized I had been given a beautiful gift of grace and I did not want it to stop. And now for the first time, I clearly understood the internal struggle I was dealing with. I finally came face to face with the ego, the bully, the rebel, the fearful terminator of joy, the disbeliever, the holder of all our negative emotions, my dark side, and the dark side of all humanity. Of course God understood where these remarks were coming from, ignored them and continued to love me. God and our Spiritual Guides understand everything, especially about the ego. I will be telling you what I learned about the ego in the pages to come.

Jesus' intention, through these books, is for all of us to begin to understand how to look within ourselves and uncover the role we are meant to play on this earth. These are His words, His message to you, His people.

Chapter Two

A Spiritual Framework to Understand Your Life

"Life is But a Dream"
The illusion we hold onto that life is reality
is due to our forgetfulness, our separation from God
We can only see what our eyes and programing tell us
There is no truth to any of it
The only truth is love.......

Indulge me; allow me to give you a spiritual framework to help you better understand yourself and life. It's not a new framework, but I believe it can help start to open your eyes, lift the veil to a new perspective, a new way to see yourself and others.

As I started my spiritual journey this truth came to me; I just started to see and understand it but never had a formal name that I could put to it. At a later date, I heard about this theory and it really helped make sense of what I was experiencing. Some call it a Soul Contract or a Pre-Birth Arrangement with God/Spirit. It is a way of coming to recognize and understand our true selves as being one with God/Spirit.

What if we imagine our soul/spirit, pre-birth, discussing a life path with God/Spirit? What if we plan out our paths in a way that is designed to provide your soul with opportunities to learn lessons of enlightenment, to evolve to higher levels of consciousness and understanding…evolving your soul, maturing it?

What if we plan everything, every detail, nuance, and event including our physical death (our soul never dies) for our journey? What if there are no coincidences or mistakes? What if we pick events; our parents and siblings and all the other people in our life to play supporting roles in helping us learn the lessons we need to learn and to understand and complete the tasks or purpose we are here to accomplish? What if we are invisibly chaperoned by other spirits/universe, as well as by people placed exactly at the right time in our life to help us achieve our goals? What if, in a sense, our soul creates a dream? I have come to accept all of this as truth.

Look at your life as a book. You are the main character in the story and everyone else is an actor (unknowingly) in supporting roles to bring love, miracles, tragedy, adversity, suffering and awakening on your path to enlightenment. Each person is actually a part of you that you do not recognize. Each may be reflecting a wound that is unhealed, our stubborn ego, or maybe a beautiful attribute that you have not embraced. We all have many different facets to our being. They all reflect parts of you that are not in your awareness because you are living unconsciously and are unknowingly projecting all of your different feelings, thoughts, attitudes, beliefs, character traits (both positive and negative) onto everyone and everything around you.

Projection is a product of the ego. One of my core beliefs about myself from childhood was that it was my job to make others happy but that I was a failure at this and never really could make people happy. Upon meeting other people, my core assumption was that if they were unhappy then I needed to make them happy if I wanted them to love me or like me. In my mind, I would then project and act on what I thought would make someone happy, what they might like or what they might need; I would try too hard and overdo, yet none of it was true. My ego was centered on a set of false beliefs about what my purpose in life was, i.e. to make other people happy, which is part of the "story" of who I am. The truth is, we really can't make anyone happy but ourselves.

At that point in my life, I didn't understand this truth. As a result, I always felt that I was a failure. Constantly seeing myself as a failure unconsciously caused intense and deeply embedded feelings of shame, guilt and aloneness. I was unknowingly caught up in an interactive web of assumptions, projections, beliefs, thoughts, feelings, patterns that resulted in self defeating behaviors. As long as we remain spiritually 'unconscious' we are all caught up in our own self destructive web.

Another example of projection would be: I am angry so I unconsciously project my anger onto everyone else, and thus see everyone else as angry. I view my truth in others facial expressions (affect) and behaviors that I hide from myself due to being disconnected from myself and unconscious.

The feeling of anger is internal to me yet the way I see, sense, or perceive others is a reflection of what I am feeling. Many times our feelings are hiding in our unconscious, in our dark side. We have all become so expert at suppressing our feelings and detaching from ourselves that we don't really even know the feelings exist.

Since I had been victimized as a young girl I developed a core belief that I am a victim. Even though this was a core belief, I wasn't consciously aware of it. It had become part of my ego's fear but it was hiding in my unconscious, my dark side. I then unconsciously assumed that everyone was out to get me or victimize me in some way. These unconscious beliefs affected all of my relationships with family and friends. It affected the basic way that I interacted with the world at large, how I viewed my work, how I interacted with acquaintances, even down to decisions about where I would shop, etc. If a situation didn't go the way I wanted I assumed that I was somehow being victimized. Of course, most of the time that wasn't the case.

When you are in a state of spiritual unconsciousness, everything you see on the outside of you is a reflection of some part of you, but not in your awareness. If you see anger, there is anger inside of you. If you see fear or hate, it's a part of you also and many of these feelings belong to the ego. All of this happens when we are unconscious and it is why we need to wake up and stay present so we stop creating and projecting negative things outside of us and into our own world.

Each one of us is 100% responsible for our reality and what we see on the outside. We are the creator. So what we think and believe in our core is what we create and see outside of us. We will bring to us what we think about ourselves. We are creating without even trying or understanding we are creating. We give life to our thoughts and beliefs, which will be positive or negative energy. We make our life a beautiful light or we make it dark. This is a very difficult concept; however, when you start to see it happening and know it, you have seen the true reality. This is the difference between how two individuals can see one situation from completely different perspectives. Each person has their own reality.

Each person and event is a crucial part of our awakening. Each is designed to teach us something about ourselves, about the illusion of life, and help our souls evolve. Our spiritual journey is a path that can lead us back to our soul, heal our wounds and help us understand the truths of what we have experienced. Along the way, we can learn how to forgive, to live and love in the present (consciously awake), and discover who we truly are.

So we have our Soul Contract or Pre-Birth plan and we are born into our human form, we incarnate and then we forget. But life has a way of taking over, and inevitably along the way we are hurt and wounded, typically in childhood, and the karmic lessons become entrenched and activated. We are now living in a world programed by our family, our family history, and by the society and culture in which we live. We are now being led by our ego, cultivating a story of who we are and reacting with patterns to the wounds we have suffered within this lifetime and past lives. There becomes a gap between our ego and our soul. Dr. Margaret Paul would call this gap our wounded adult self who lives unconsciously led by the ego. Margaret explains that this wounded self was part of our soul at one time but broke away from it as it experienced wounds in our childhood.

The only way for our soul to learn its lessons is through witnessing our humanness and evolving toward a deeper consciousness, a heightened maturity. Our soul is always within, quietly watching and waiting, trying to help and guide us, however, the wounded adult in us is more in alignment with our ego than our soul. It does not mean that we never hear or feel our soul; we do but only on rare occasions. This is why we want to meditate, to hear the soul. As the wounded adult heals, learns lessons and evolves into a more loving adult it moves into greater alignment with our soul, or our higher self, as some call it. As the process takes place, the wounded adult part of us is actually healing and growing from a childlike immaturity to a mature loving adult capable of reuniting with its soul. The process is an evolution of love, light and wisdom. It is a life's journey if not more.

We each need to remove the veil of unconsciousness. As we lift the veil it exposes light and truth and our seeing becomes much clearer and expanded. We see both the beauty and the illusion of life and the part we play in it. Life is magic and perfection; in fact, it is enchanting.

Unfortunately, as we're growing up and even through our adulthood, we are not given clear paths to help us understand this or recognize that the Kingdom even exists.

The veil is lifted in increments, moments, days, and years at a time. Each increment is perfectly timed and is given to you exactly when you are ready for another divine dance with God/Spirit that will take you a step closer to your ultimate performance…finding and fulfilling the purpose of your life.

I cannot lift your veil and you cannot lift mine, but we can be there to embrace each others' awakening with arms stretched out with love and grace to welcome each other home as kindred spirits and to respect each individual's own process and journey.

Everyone and everything we encounter in our life's journey is an actor or planned event with a specific role to play in our life. Everything we experience, feel, or witness is a performance by others to help wake us up and lift the veil of our unconsciousness another increment, so healing can occur within. These are blessings and we should be grateful for the opportunities to grow.

We need to embrace those events and people, past and present, that have caused us to experience our internal conflicts and pain, for they have appeared in our lives to help us spiritually grow and evolve. Their performance is divinely orchestrated and executed, as is yours.

You have your path and I have mine and, of course, so does everyone else. Each person is following her/his own plan, the dream that her/his soul created. We are part of their learning experiences and they are part of ours. We are all mirror projections of each other. We reflect the ego, our wounds and souls to each other. We are all one, having a collective consciousness experience together. Our job is to awaken, heal, remember that we are divine, and reconnect with our soul so we can continue on to fulfill the purpose of our story and our life here on earth.

I know this is complicated and that's okay. I would have had trouble with this had I not experienced it. Your enlightenment or awakening happens at exactly the right time, as planned, when you are ready for it. Be patient, keep alert and stay conscious.

A SPIRITUAL FRAMEWORK TO UNDERSTAND YOUR LIFE

Journal Entry 2/27/2016
With Jesus

Jesus: It is part of being human to experience profound grief when we live unconsciously. We live unconsciously if we experience our lives in the context of our ego's programming. To the extent that we are able to avoid our ego's programming and live consciously in the present, this does not happen. *Me:* But many people have not been able to process all of the grief they've experienced in life. *Jesus:* Yes, but life is an illusion. *Me:* That illusion starts when we are first wounded in childhood? *Jesus:* Yes, Debbie, it starts when we are born and becomes entrenched when we are first wounded. Experiencing grief is a part of the human condition. Grief is not part of your spirit. Your true spiritual self doesn't know or experience grief or misery. *Me:* What is the role of misery in life? *Jesus:* Experiencing misery, pain, and grief are all lessons that can stimulate spiritual learning and an expansion of one's soul. *Me:* So a spirit has to take on human form in order for a soul to evolve? *Jesus:* Yes, that is correct, it is the only way. *Me:* So that is why it takes so many lifetimes? *Jesus:* Yes. *Me:* Does the grief ever go away? *Jesus:* As you transcend the emotions of the ego, your human experience of grief will dissipate. *Me:* So this brings us back to our original discussion on death. *Jesus:* Yes, experiencing grief is like death in a sense. To experience that much misery, is like a death. *Me:* Is that why some people commit suicide? *Jesus:* Yes, their misery is death itself. *Me:* So we don't have to die physically in order to, in some sense, die spiritually. *Jesus:* That is what the unconscious state is, misery and spiritual death. *Me:* But I was unconscious and thought I was happy. *Jesus:* That is just *being in a state of denial of the grief and misery.* **Me:** *So our job as humans is to transcend misery.* **Jesus:** *Yes.* **Me:** *Does that ever occur?* **Jesus:** *No.* **Me:** *Why?* **Jesus:** *Because we have not lived enough lives.* **Me:** *How many lifetimes does that take?* **Jesus:** *It goes on forever. But, then you would not have experienced all the wonderful things in your life, such as your children.* **Me:** *So although there is misery there is much joy too, it's the yin and yang. Grief then is also a disconnection from our self and God?* **Jesus:** *Yes, that is the ultimate grief that we keep repeating in our life as a human. It is our disconnection from the life force and that feels like death, misery, grief.* **Me:** *So, somehow, we have a certain innate understanding of all this?* **Jesus:** *Yes, but it is part of the illusion because, in reality, we are never detached from God; we just believe we are, we have forgotten.* **Me:** *That is why it is the soul's goal to have us awaken, so that we can reconnect back to our soul/our highest which is connected to God by going through whatever lessons were learned in that lifetime?* **Jesus:** *Yes.*

Chapter Three

Keep Going Inside

*The separation from me has caused
great confusion, aloneness and emptiness
I never left you. You left me
I wait patiently for your return
My beautiful child*

As you keep exploring, you will find patterns of belief systems that belong to your ego programing and life events you have experienced. You will see reoccurring events throughout your life that trigger the same painful issues. They are part of your lessons that need to be addressed, healed, forgiven and released.

Let's say, for example, that you have a fear of abandonment or rejection. Your life will be filled with events and people that keep triggering that fear. Fear of abandonment and rejection has been one of my deep core beliefs that kept showing up in different areas of my life, including understanding how I actually abandoned and reject my own self. On a deeper level, I believe this comes from a very old and deeply ingrained generational feeling of being detached from God. These events and people are being brought into your life so that you will have the opportunity to confront your fear and your belief. They will keep showing up in your life until you finally understand your fear and heal it. It can be a tedious and exhausting process. Please recognize that everyone in your life and everything surrounding you in your life are giving you messages about yourself and, without realizing it, you are doing the same thing for others as well.

I know this is a lot to absorb, but try it out for a while. Everyone who does something irritating or that you dislike is role modeling a part of you that you don't see or refuse to acknowledge. The funny thing is, the people are completely unaware that they are role modeling for you; they are just being themselves. They are showing you that part of you that you keep hidden from yourself. The negative thoughts and feelings you have from viewing someone else's behaviors are a mirror to show you something about you that needs to be healed. They are showing you something you need to acknowledge, confront and heal. It could be something you do to others or something you do to yourself within your own mind or quietly. It might be something you think to yourself about others but don't verbalize or you might think or act towards yourself.

Example: If you feel someone is doing something or saying something that makes you feel angry, insecure, guilty, or judgmental, it is because you are unconsciously witnessing yourself in that person and/or they are helping you bring up feelings that need to be healed because something is underlying them deep within you. Your reaction to others is actually a reaction to your own self who does exactly the same thing but you do not have the awareness that you act the same way. On some unconscious level you do know you have the same traits within yourself and you feel guilt or shame about them, but you keep them hidden from yourself, your shadow side. Your strong reaction is a sign that it is your problem and you need to investigate it.

Now of course, the persons who are role modeling for you are just being themselves and have no idea of the part they are playing in your life. Understand also that you are doing the same for them. As you begin to find your truth, you will begin to have this awareness about yourself.

Maybe you engaged in a certain behavior or experienced something at a different time in your life and you repressed the feelings. Negative feelings and uncomfortable situations keep happening when you see others engaging in the same behavior or see a similar scenario. It can even be on the news or an event happening in the world. Your reaction typically means that something needs to be healed within you. The more you are not judging the insights you are gaining, the more awareness will come to you.

The same is true when you see people who have attributes that you really admire. You have those too, but maybe unaware of them as well; you keep them hidden from you. All of the things that you judge in other people are the same things that you do. Be careful what you think or say because you are actually judging yourself. You have to find humor in all of this because it is so completely hypocritical. We all do it and we do it because we are human and have an ego that keeps us asleep and unconscious.

You will become more aware of how this process works as you come to more fully understand that we are all unconsciously asleep at the wheel of life and have no clue that we are asleep, living unconsciously with our ego in charge. It is the story of the life we created before we were born and then forgot. In some ways it sounds like a sci-fi movie where everyone is in a trance until they are eventually awakened and see the truth.

This life is just a dream. It is the life we created for our dream state. Our spirit is dreaming as a collective consciousness that it took on a human form on the planet earth. That dream is just an illusion, however, it is an essential part of the soul's evolution to live in this illusion and forget it is a dream and that we are Divine. Everything that we experience appears real and feels real just like it does in a dream or a nightmare at times. We are creating the journey that we experience in this dream state with all of the events that teach us the lessons our soul needs to learn. We simply need to awaken to learn those lessons. It is our job to awaken and explore our pre-arranged lessons by reconnecting to Spirit. We are not doing this alone, we each have a master spiritual teacher within and many spiritual guides working with us.

I had taken that last paragraph out when I first edited these books because I was struggling with believing the concept of a dream myself. Even though Jesus dictated all of the words in these books, during my many edits I struggled with the idea of including the paragraph in that it seemed so incredibly hard to believe. Jesus and I had a discussion about life being a dream at the time and He told me I have dreamed everything that I have experienced in life, and because of all of the negative emotional and physical memories I had, it made it very difficult for me to believe. Jesus again told me, these experiences did not really happen and, in the end, I decided to include the paragraph as it was given to me due to my faith and trust in the information I had been given. I did this even though I was having trouble digesting the whole concept myself. In fact, I rebelled against it for quite a while because I felt grief over the fact that I and everyone else had experienced so much suffering for seemingly no reason.

I have now come to a place in my journey where I am able to understand and integrate this into my own process. My ego did not want to accept it, but the truth is, I do not know everything. Not everything makes sense because we do not have all the answers. This is faith.

Most of us are not 'getting' the lessons because our ego is still in charge. We are unconscious and are stuck in our mind-chatter of thoughts, feelings and programing. Sometimes we might understand a lesson, but do not always get to internalize it because we keep getting pulled back into that unconscious state. The goal is to wake up, become conscious and present, stay conscious and present for ever-longer periods of time, and start seeing the truth about the illusion of life and the ego's role.

So, some of you might be reading this and have not yet woken up, but you feel somehow that something needs to change within you or that there is something more about you or life and can't put your finger on it. Hearing this explanation can seem pretty far-fetched and difficult to relate to. Nevertheless, it is the truth, as I have experienced it. As you become more awake and progress through different levels of consciousness, you will come to understand these truths as well.

Barbara De Angelis has a great chapter about earth in her book 'Soul Shifts' where she describes how the earth is moving and rotating in our solar system, getting pulled along by the Sun within the Milky Way Galaxy in a vast unending universe. If you look at this truth, you can start to understand that living on a planet in the solar system sounds far-fetched but we believe it. One might ask how is this possible? What are we? How did we get here? These questions have been asked since the beginning of time, but there are no clear answers. When I started to awaken I remember driving in my car and looking at the sky and everything around me saying, what am I and what is all of this? I am living on a planet in outer space in a tiny solar system and none of it makes sense!

It is all an illusion. We all share the same starting point for our dream, which is that we are born as humans here on earth. From that point onward, everyone's story is their own yet we are having a collective consciousness experience.

What I have found out is that we are all Spirit. This is the wisdom I have been given by Jesus. "The earth and being human is the soul's playground of learning and evolving. As the heavens are infinite so is the knowledge and wisdom to learn. This is why we keep incarnating; it is the job of our spirit/soul. Our ego is part of being human and it gives us unending opportunities to experience pain and suffering for our soul to witness without ever being harmed, to evolve and grow life after life."

Chapter Four

Let This Book Re-Parent You Spiritually

You are a beautiful blessing
You are not broken & never have been
You are a perfect reflection of God

We are born with the knowledge and support of everything we need to know. Unfortunately, as we grow up, no one teaches us how to extract this knowledge from within. If you are lucky, you may find your inner knowledge through meditation, or prayer, or simply being quiet enough to hear God/Spirit's word. There is no special alchemy involved in finding your inner truth. It is simply just connecting to your higher consciousness and the rest will reveal itself over time. Your ego, however, will keep denying the truth you receive over and over again. It will keep you from accepting it and keep you focused outwardly.

Even so, if you make room for quiet time, deep breathing, meditation, you will eventually hear the voice of wisdom or find an understanding within your heart of what God/Spirit is sharing with you. God/Spirit/your higher consciousness (which is another name for your higher self, soul or spirit) is talking to you all the time; we just don't hear it. We hear so much of the noise that surrounds us in our everyday lives, but we're not used to listening to what's quietly going on inside ourselves. Listen to your intuition. Once you start to experience this, you'll find love that is so overwhelming it is pure bliss. Sometimes you will find that you don't want to leave this internal sacred world because you feel so safe and loved.

There can be many paths to reaching your higher consciousness. One path is through 'guided imagery' where you have a visual awareness, a seeing as with your mind's eye, your inner eye or imagination. Having a visual image of your spiritual guidance can accelerate your growth toward higher consciousness. It enhances your abilities and helps you feel even more connected to God/Spirit.

The imagery that I use personally came from Dr. Margaret Paul's book: Do I Have to Give Up Me to be Loved By God? The book contains a guided imagery on page 177 written by Dr. Erika Chopich that is a very powerful tool that helps you make a visual connection to Spirit. I have used this tool myself and it is what connected me to my spiritual guidance, Jesus. I use this tool with all my clients as well and it helps get them started on their spiritual journey.

What is unique about this visual is it allows a person to connect through whatever belief system they may have. It has no religious connotations to it. It's all about divine love and light and learning how to love one's self. Someone will have to read the text of Erika's guidance to you. It's up to you, as the listener, to decide how you define 'divine' as you relax, breathe, close your eyes and use your imagination to get started.

For some, the strength of the visual component is in seeing Spirit, love, and light. For me, it was my first awareness that I had the ability to see, hear and feel spirit. For others, they may not see but they can always hear directly through their heart since that is where God speaks to us. Erika's guided imagery is indeed a blessing. It is clearly a divine gift to aid in helping people connect and go deeper in their personal transformation and understanding of the truth about their connection with the universe…that all things are actually one. There is no separation between the universe and everything in it.

My first experience with this type of meditation was at one of Margaret's workshops in September of 2014 at Kripalu Yoga Center in Stockbridge Massachusetts. I had never been to a personal development experiential workshop before, only professional development, and felt like a fish out of water in a yoga center. I had never practiced yoga before either. What a blessing to experience both of these new things together. Margaret read the guided imagery to us and I immediately envisioned myself sitting on the edge of my friend's pool. Water is extremely grounding for me. A pool or beach is a place where I feel relaxed and connected. The meditation is about learning to love yourself and an invitation for your spiritual guidance. All of a sudden, a thirty-something male figure appeared sitting next to me, shoulder length brown wavy hair, dark eyes wearing a pair of jeans and a tee shirt. Next to him was what I thought to be a kind of Aztec blanket, but was really a prayer shawl. I learned later this will become my prayer shawl. The person felt very safe and loving.

As the meditation continued on I was floating on a raft and he joined me in the water and suddenly several of my younger wounded children appeared in my arms lying on the raft with me. I was dumbfounded, a little scared, didn't know what was happening and didn't know what to do. It didn't make sense, however, it was happening, and it was like a movie playing in my mind. He took my arms and wrapped them around my younger selves (I will talk more about rescuing these abandon parts of me in another volume). He was teaching me how to love myself and the healing that occurred started me on my transformation. I cried and cried from the healing love that I was feeling; it was profound. At first I thought it was this man healing me but as I continued on my journey I recognized that I was being taught that I can heal myself. We all have the ability to heal ourselves emotionally, and I found out later that we can heal ourselves physically as well. This was my first awareness of the enormous power we each have within us.

I was so confused from what I experienced since it was all very new to me, I had no reference to compare it to. At Kripalu they were selling blankets that looked like the one that the man brought with him. I had to buy one (a green colored one) since it stood out as such an important piece of my meditation.

I talked to my husband about what I experienced when I returned home and he thought the man sounded like Jesus and the blanket was actually a prayer shawl. My inner child kept telling me it was Jesus but I could not wrap my head around it, I resisted. Why would Jesus show up in my meditation? Being raised Jewish I thought…well Jesus was Jewish so maybe that's why…but it took me a long time until I felt settled with the notion. It was my ego that was unsettled trying to make sense of what happened instead of just accepting what was.

Your spiritual guidance knows everything about you, what you are going to do, what you need, where you see yourself as broken. The blanket was symbolic because I needed to do a lot of safety building within myself and with Jesus and needed a lot of reassurance. Jesus had brought me a new security blanket to help me hold onto Him as I started my spiritual journey because my ego often blocked my connection. I am sure this blanket has other symbolism but I have not unraveled it all yet. Everything that was happening within me was so foreign and I did not know who to talk to about it. I never let anyone in to help me before.

After returning home from Kripalu, I meditated and practiced sitting with Jesus daily and it always felt so peaceful and loving. I started to use this meditation tool with my clients and the majority of them identified their own spiritual guidance and started on their own spiritual awakening. One day, I thought to myself, why don't Jesus and I speak to one another? I heard a voice inside of me that said, "Just say hello to him." I said "Hello" and he responded! I could hear him and carry on a conversation! The teaching and loving that I have received from Him has been such a blessing.

Recognition of the true nature of our connection to the universe leads to the understanding that we are all pure energy, love and light. We have always been, and always will be. Because we are all just pure energy, there are no differences between people/souls. There is no race, gender, religion, or any of the countless other things that ego and programming uses to separate us. Everything that is alive or not alive is part of us because everything is energy, or matter, or vibration.

This understanding doesn't exist in the unconscious state that we live in…the one controlled by our ego. Coming to realize and accept this will take time as you keep transcending into higher states of consciousness. The ego will always continue to hold you back, which is spiritually purposeful and that is why we call it a journey.

As you meditate and use the skills we discuss you will see there are different levels of awakening to greater wisdom and knowledge over time. Each level will come to you when you are ready for it. You are actually being prepared for these different levels of awakening through this Spiritual re-parenting from your guidance. You will only receive what you are ready for. This is why your connection to God/Spirit through your higher consciousness is so important. This is where the understanding of your own true self and how to master your self begins.

Your higher consciousness is a place for you to learn the truth of who you are, not who you think you are. It is where you actually learn right from wrong in a much different way, a way that isn't programed by ego, family, events or society. It is a place for all healing to occur, to understand forgiveness, gratitude, blessings, grace, honor, love and light. It is also a safe place for us to mature emotionally and evolve spiritually since our ego and our souls can be extremely immature and many of us get stuck emotionally in a child mindset of judgment, anger, fear, frustration, entitlement, expectation, I want, I should, you should, etc.

Spirit gives you all of this knowledge in the most loving way. Therefore, the love is transformative. There is no judgment, only light. This is where trust begins. For when you understand that there is only love, light and truth to help you evolve to your highest, you begin to let go of fear and mistrust as you come to see and feel true safety for the first time in your life. Most of my spiritual growth and healing has come from meditation during which Jesus and God teach me the lessons that I need to learn. Many of the lessons have to do with there being no hierarchy among God, Jesus, Spirit or yourself or anyone else for that matter. We are all equal. We are not to worship or idolize anything. You are God, the great I AM. This was very difficult for me as I have never felt Spiritual Love before and we are taught to worship through programing. Please see below a small out-take from a journal entry.

Journal Entry
A visual meditation with God
1/26/2016

Me: *(I had fallen to the ground on my knees at God's feet in awe of the blessings he has bestowed onto me). I worship the ground you walk on, I feel so loved and cared for.* **God:** *You need to rise my child, you do not need to kneel at my feet. You are to sit along side me. Stand up tall, you are a gift, you are a beautiful blessing yourself. You must remember who you are.* **Me:** *I don't remember.*
God: *It will come, allow it so you can manifest into who you truly are, who I made you to be.*

Chapter Five

The Kingdom of Heaven is Within Us and Always Has Been

Blessed O' Lord, King of the Universe
Please allow me to hear and know the love
and majesty that awaits me
For without knowing this I can never come to be
who you blessed me to be

The Kingdom of Heaven is within us and always has been. The magnitude of spiritual unconditional love and acceptance that is available to us is profound.

Today, we are told to turn inward to listen and meditate to find this profound love. Most of us cannot sit still or quiet our minds long enough to do this. So, how do we begin? First of all, there is no perfect place or way to meditate. You can meditate anywhere as long as you have a space in which you can be quiet and still. Of course, being in a beautiful natural setting is always appealing and can help you relax, but it's not a necessity. You don't have to sit a certain way or have your hands a certain way (mudras), although, they can help you focus more and some people are drawn to the more traditional meditation methods. You do not need special clothing, crystals, set up an alter or go to a mountain top. If you want to do these things it is fine just not necessary.

All the power is within each one of us, not outside of us. I was someone who thought I had to have all the right equipment, clothing, music, etc. to accomplish meditating and it is not true. I have meditated in all kinds of places, sitting in my work chair, in my little grandson's bed, in a hotel and on the beach to name a few.

My favorite place is in my bed where I am propped up against a bunch of pillows so I am slightly reclining with my legs stretched out in front of me. I turn off my phone so I am not interrupted. I play music that helps center me, such as, Ashana with Thomas Barquee - Jewels of Silence and then close my eyes and start taking deep breaths and before long I am in a deep relaxed state. Because I use visual imagery some times I have a specific agenda I want to discuss and understand more. Other times I let my higher self take me wherever she wants me to go. I also keep a journal near me so I can reflect on what I learned after I've completed my meditation.

There is no set amount of time to meditate. If you have 5 minutes it is better than nothing. My typical meditations can last anywhere from 15 minutes to 1½ hours. The longer you can stay in a meditative state the more healing and teaching can occur. If I am working on healing my body from something or rejuvenating myself than I will meditate for 1½ hours. An easy place for you to start your journey to discover the truth within is simply to find a comfortable spot to sit, breathe, and listen. The goal is to learn how to listen with your heart, not just with your ears, for that is where spirit speaks to you. Do the best you can to quiet your mind. Breathe in deeply through your nose and then exhale slowly but forcefully through your mouth. Continue to breathe, gently, peacefully in your own natural rhythm between each deep breath.

Notice any sensations that come up within you and just observe. Don't judge them; just be aware of them as if they were something separate from you. Don't label your thoughts as good or bad, just be aware, as if you were watching them float by, drifting in to notice them and watching them leave. Mostly all thinking is the ego. Continue to breathe and as you do so, let go of control, thoughts, and feelings.

Imagine that as you breathe out, each feeling or thought is leaving through your exhalation. Continue to do this until you are calm inside. Don't be afraid of any of the feelings or thoughts that arise; they won't harm you even if they are negative. There is nothing to think about at this moment, 'You are mine' says your beautiful inner soul/spirit. Your soul is quietly waiting, waiting to be rediscovered so it can love you and provide you with wisdom (light) for your life's journey.

Mastering meditation takes time and practice but eventually you will be able to sit still and calm your mind. Some days will be better than others. Don't give up. Don't get discouraged. Don't beat yourself up and tell yourself that you aren't making progress; you are. You may not see your progress each day, but it's there. Believe and be patient and loving with yourself. As I was learning how to do this, I also found that during the day it was very useful to take deep cleansing breaths every couple of hours even when you are not meditating. At times, I still experience interference from my ego while meditating. It happens to all of us. Don't worry about it. Just keep bringing yourself back to center. With practice you will eventually achieve enough internal quietness to begin making real progress.

What you are striving for is the ability to see with your mind's eye (images or similar to watching a movie with you in it), or hear through your inner ear, and/or know and hear through your heart. Your heart knows how to translate what you are hearing through it. You just understand what is spoken to you without hearing a word. It is the ability to discern between your ego self-talk and the voice of your soul/Spirit. Peace will only come to you when you can hear the soft inner voice of your soul or Spiritual guide. You will know the difference when your ego and its programing is talking to you through your self-talk; it will not be the same peace.

Just an aside, I have the ability to journal and hear spirit talking with me at the same time, I do not need to meditate to accomplish this. What I found through my own process is that it became easy not to meditate because of this ability. My ego felt very comfortable just channeling while journaling and I was not meditating enough. There is a huge benefit that I get from meditating that I cannot duplicate while channeling. The visual imagery impacts me in a much different way and the nourishment my body receives is enormous. Therefore, I try to meditate daily.

Do you want to hear your love story of who you really are and why you are here? It's a very different story than the one you have believed and have been listening to…the story your ego has been telling you your whole life. Your story of truth and divinity is completely different.

Our ego is part of being human; it is our false sense of self. As one of my client's has called it, the ego is "the voice of our delusions." It helped us survive as we evolved as a species. It sees itself as our protector, always watching out to deflect us from pain, real or imagined. It is what always keeps us worried and in fear of some kind of extinction or emotional, physical or spiritual pain. Understand that your soul has nothing to do with your ego and your ego has nothing to do with your soul; they are completely separate. My personal belief is that the Ego has a Divine purpose. It is an indispensable part of us acting as an obstacle course that our souls must navigate and overcome in order for us to fully awaken as creators and come into the love that is rightly ours. One could look at it as a video game in which we need to learn all the nuances, booby traps, snags and obstructions to win the game. The Ego is like a giant web of beliefs, programing, experiences, thinking, feeling, behaviors that turn into patterns that are all interconnected, like a matrix. It has created the performance and appearance we show others. Ego influences how we react to situations. We need to simply accept that our ego exists. We cannot change it. It is a part of us that needs to be embraced. We just need to stop listening to it and stop letting it control our lives. We need to unplug from it and stop feeding into the thoughts and patterns that it produces. Otherwise, we will continue to suffer by the hand of the ego, and the suffering is insidious.

If you look at what is underneath everything we worry about there is a fear of suffering. This just came to my own attention in a greater way. I was examining my thoughts and suffering is attached to almost everything, such as, "what if I eat the wrong thing", I will gain weight, get sick, I will suffer. What if I don't have enough income, I am afraid to say no to something, why do I have to work so hard, what if I can't make it to work on time, why does it take so much time to take care of myself, why do I have to do everything, I have to think about what to make for dinner, again, why do I have to worry what happens if the laundry doesn't get done, should I put gas in my car now or later, what happens if I don't see my family for the holidays, why am I so happy, why am I so tired, why does my body ache, what happens if I can't exercise today, I can go on and on. At the end of each one of these questions is "then I am going to suffer somehow." These are just a few things that go through my mind and I know that they are representative of a lot of other people's thoughts.

Everything from the ego is a fear about suffering. We are not suffering but we believe we are suffering or going to suffer, it is all part of the illusion. Our lens or perspective in how we view things in our life and others is slanted towards suffering and then believe suffering is intolerable.

This is our great challenge. We give our ego immense power and control because no one taught us how to discipline it or dismiss it. We give it power unknowingly, unconsciously. When we live through our ego we live a life of spiritual unconsciousness. We live our lives as though we are asleep in our own dream world, going through each day believing that we are living and functioning in reality...but the truth is, we are not.

The truth is that we live in the illusion of life. We live in a story that we have made up about ourselves. We created our storyline based upon what we were taught by our family and society as we grew up and by our experience of life from the moment of our birth. This is our programming, and there is precious little truth to much of it since so much of it is based on unrealistic ideas, fears, prejudices, emotions, etc. that have been passed on to us by others.

I'm not talking about the practicalities of life that we have been taught, such as not sticking your hand into a fire, or jumping off a bridge. I'm talking about your ego, your programming...who you are, how you should act, what expectations you should have for yourself and those around you, your purpose in life, how to be happy or what should make you happy or sad. These are stories that have been developed culturally and societally and have been passed down generationally since the beginning of time. Our ego then adds to the story with its own irrational ideas of how it will keep us safe and help us receive love.

I was shocked when I finally stopped to listen to the ego-chatter in my head. I was also appalled by much of what it thinks. The busy-ness of my day-to-day life camouflaged this chatter to an extent but in reality, it was affecting me on so many levels. One of the main jobs of the ego is to keep us so busy in our head that we are not able to stay present, listen or feel. For most of my years I was a walking head disconnected from my body...and certainly my soul. Now it is time to get in your body (your heart) and out of your head. This is not an easy transition but one that needs to be done. This is a long process that I continue to work on daily.

This is what can come as you build a connection to your higher self as you meditate. Visual meditation is like watching myself in a movie in my mind. We all daydream and it is somewhat a similar effect.

Journal Entry 1/29/15
An in-depth conversation with my higher self... a visual meditation of walking together on the beach in the surf

Me: *Why are we here?* **HS:** *Stand still and feel the sand and water around us. It connects us to feel that we are one with the earth/universe. It is our job to treat this earth well, as it is to treat our self and others well. We are all connected and part of each other, and we are all to enjoy what God has given and created. Every person and thing on this earth is one; we are all extensions of each other. People, animals, fish, mountains, water, our homes and the things our homes are built from and everything in them come from some part of the earth. Each of us individually and all of us collectively are a whole universe, the same whole universe. We are all one. However, we separate ourselves from everyone else and everything else. It's a clannish type of separation that prevents us from seeing that we're all interconnected.*

Me: *Why do we do this?* **HS:** *Fear, lack of understanding, greed, our ego, and simply the fact of our being human. It is our job to reconnect. Our souls long to reconnect to the earth, each other and our universe. Based on our soul's journey we all go about this in different ways.*

Me: *How are we supposed to do this?* **HS:** *We walk our journey and discover our purpose through love. Our soul is meant to share love and to remind everyone of God's beauty. We do this by being strong, healthy, loving, caring, kind to ourselves, to others and to our surroundings. Our purpose is to love. It is the purpose of all souls to love. By feeling God's love and showing your happiness, joy, and God given talents, you have a profound effect on others.*

Chapter Six

The Blessings of Programing

You are never separate from your divinity
It is housed within you
All you need to do is call on it
Spirit will always guide you
But you must be open to listening
You are never alone....

Luckily, our soul is also programed to remember where we came from and who we truly are. We understand that we have a great connection to a life force, an energy that we refer to as God, Spirit, prana, chi, love, light, universe or divinity. This is our first truth. It is reflected in the absolute love and joy we see in our babies' faces, their beautiful innocence, and the smell of God's purity and breath upon them.

We are all born with this truth. You still have that beautiful innocence and purity inside you; it is your soul. Over time, however, the world we are born into helps us forget and ultimately separates us from our first truth. For even if we do remember or feel faith or a connection to God/Spirit, we lose the ability to trust as our ego/programming takes over. So instead of being connected to our first truth, our divinity, we are now connected to the programming of our ego, culture and society.

The good news is that our first truth is always with us just like a computer or phone that can always be restored to its original factory settings. Our life journey is to wake ourselves up from the illusion of our ego storyline and find our way back to our first truth, our spiritual programing. No matter how many times I go unconscious I can always go back to my meditation and guides.

There are mechanisms built into our spiritual programming to help us or remind us to look deep within ourselves and awaken to our truth. These reminders might be life events, positive or negative, mishaps, accidents, the birth of a baby or the death of someone close to us, or even on our own deathbed. Throughout our life we will be given numerous opportunities to wake up. Unfortunately, most of these 'Aha' moments are short-lived. A moment, an hour, a few days, weeks, months, and then we fall back into the abyss of unconsciousness.

Our ego is constantly pulling us back into unconsciousness, into a trance. It is always fighting for control, fighting for its own survival within the context of the storyline we/ego have constructed. Our ego does not like to stay present and does not understand or trust our soul. It will not relinquish control without a fight. Our ego is so very tricky and smart. It will have you think negative or fearful things about yourself and others that will distract you from your innate spiritual knowledge that wants to lead you back to your first truth. There is also the Spiritual Ego that makes believe it is being spiritual. Wow, let me tell you how my Spiritual Ego will make believe it is Jesus, God, my Higher Self. At first, this Spiritual Ego would confuse me and get me sidetracked. But now, after lots of hard work, I've gotten to the point where (most of the time) I can recognize when it is trying to lure me in.

If you step back and look at all of your different internal and external programming, it's no wonder that we gradually slip into spiritual unconsciousness. Ego is the master manipulator that makes us believe that we can trust no one but ourselves. The truth is that many of us don't even trust ourselves. The ego is all about controlling us and everyone else around us to make us feel safe and comfortable. It manipulates us by being very nice or through power, anger, passivity and persuasiveness. When we are in our ego we can be happy at times and feel like our life is wonderful… and it may well be, at least on the surface. We may have financial security, good relationships, and a career that we enjoy. Even so, we can still be totally disconnected from our self and others. I have experienced this first hand. We may be completely unaware that this is even happening. If we aren't completely unconscious we may experience a fleeting moment that whispers in our ear… 'Am I truly happy, truly fulfilled?' 'Of course you are' says our ego, and off we go back into the abyss.

Chapter Seven

What Is It We Truly Want? What's Missing?

God has made sure you lack nothing within

We want to be happy, loved, peaceful, purposeful and free! The universe is set up to constantly give us signals that we are asleep/unconscious and that we need to wake up from our storyline. The problem is that we now keep perpetuating our storyline because we are not conscious and are not working to heal our wounds. As a result, we keep creating more wounds, more suffering, more problematic events in our lives. We are manifesting all of this. There are blessings and miracles built into our story that should make us wonder whether there is something more to life than what we currently see or understand. Questions arise, but then we let go of them, they slip through our fingers and ego let's them quietly drift away…or we get stuck in the 'why's'.

Making sense of this earthly life can drive one insane. Nothing makes sense, and yet we spend so much of our time seeking explanations for why things happen the way they happen. Sometimes we get stuck for years trying to understand a single or multiple events. This is our ego. It needs to have answers and is blind to the truth that there are no answers. I myself had spent years trying to understand why I experienced certain things in my life. All this did is cause me not to accept and process what happened, it kept me from healing and forgiving. Some of us are asleep/unconscious and living out a nightmare of a story. We are suffering even though everything may appear okay on the outside, but it's not on the inside. We cannot evolve until we wake up and become conscious and then we can change/alter our story.

Even when a thought creeps in that maybe the ego isn't really in control, it usually just perpetuates more ego-based thinking, due to it refusing to accept 'what is.' To accept 'what is' means that the ego is defeated and this will bring up grief, loss, shame, guilt and anger and punish you with more control. It is part of the obstacle course I mentioned earlier.

Our ego is desperate to survive, remain safe, and get love and control. It cannot accept that it has no real answers or that it has done something wrong without bringing up negative feelings, blaming or being judgmental. There is no other hypercritical (or hypocritical) fool like the ego. It knows everything and can't wait to tell everyone. We have all seen others full of their egotistical selves and, if we are truthful, we have seen ourselves that way as well. Even if we do not make fools of ourselves on the outside, our inner self believes it knows what others are thinking, feeling, and what is really 'best' for the other person. We are constantly reading other people's lives without having any insight into our own. This is at the core of unloving behavior directed toward ourselves and others.

The ego is the source of all of our problems, yet it is a part of us that is not going away and is purposeful. It can take a perception of an event, feeling, or thought and create a drama out of it. Think how old you are right now and how many scenarios have been played out in your mind over the years. There may have been several billion 'screenplays' written with our self as the star going from suffering to glory and back again.

WHAT IS IT WE TRULY WANT? WHAT'S MISSING?

How can I help you, you ask? Stop listening to the incessant chatter of your ego. No, it's not easy, but if you are committed and ready to work on it, it will get easier over time. Become a witness to your ego and observe its irrational beliefs and its hypercritical vigilance of yourself and others. Recognize and then refuse to follow through with behaviors based on the ego's 'thinking'. You need to get to a point where you can hear and recognize the soft inner voice of your Soul/Spirit and not be hijacked by the louder, incessant mind-chatter of your ego. Our chatter is not our thoughts, it is the ego's thoughts. Our job is to get out of our head and into our body, most specifically our heart.

You can only do this by carefully observing your thought processes. Thoughts breed feelings, and your feelings are tied to your old thoughts; it's a vicious cycle and it is automatic. Don't despair; don't fight or resist. Our ego is what it is, and it's not going away. However, dismissing or letting go of the thoughts will take away their power. Observe your thoughts and the feelings they produce (mindfulness), understand where they are coming from, feel them and then let them go. We need to do this over and over and over again daily until we are only giving attention to our Soul/Spirit's voice. However, our feelings are always trying to tell us something needs attention inside, something that needs to be healed, so we do need to be thoughtful about our feelings, even if they seem irrational.

Don't set a timeline; it won't work. Accessing your Soul/Spirit's voice happens on its own timeline. You can't force the process; you can't accelerate it past what you are ready for. I want to emphasize this because we're all so used to creating deadlines. There are no deadlines in the spiritual realm. God/Spirit knows the timeline; it's nothing you need to worry about. When you continue to trust that your life has already been planned, then you don't have to focus on deadlines. As you may have heard before, everything is exactly the way it is supposed to be.

Chapter Eight

Life in the Fast Lane

*Place your hand in mine
and allow yourself to be quiet
For it is only then will you see the truth about
Yourself, Love & Light*

It's time to get off of the merry-go-round of life; otherwise the spiritual growth you are seeking won't get off the ground. We spend so much time trying to race against the clock that we lose focus on ourselves and what we are here for. Taking time for ourselves is a must in order to do this work. We've all been programed to not take time for ourselves and that everyone/everything else comes first. If we do take some time for ourselves, we go to the gym or a bar, or pick up some hobby so that we're always distracted. This does not mean you shouldn't have hobbies or interests. The time for ourselves that I'm talking about is time invested in total quiet and inner reflection.

How do you carve out time for total quiet, whether it's to meditate, journal, or do a quiet task to allow feelings, thoughts, and spirit speak to you? Most people feel guilty doing this. Most of us feel that taking time for ourselves is selfish. It is not selfish; that's only what you've been programed to believe. I know before

I awakened I never liked spending quiet time with myself I'd rather socialize. There were many reasons for this and they had to do with my wounds not being healed yet and not feeling comfortable being alone. I kept myself busy so I would not have to spend quiet time by myself. Now, I love my alone time.

Most of us have never witnessed someone taking quiet time for her/himself…quiet time to just be. You'll be astounded when you start to understand how all of your thoughts are programed and generated by what you've been taught by family, society, by what you've heard, what you've observed from others, and your own irrational beliefs. Every thought is based on some preconceived notion that has no basis in reality. In order to be able to begin to see this, you have to force yourself to make space for quiet time and get past the internal resistance from your ego. Don't get frustrated. You will not be able to do this consistently on a daily basis at first. In fact, the process of learning how to get beyond your ego can take years. I know this isn't what you want to hear but it's the truth. Learning to overcome the internal resistance from your ego takes a lot of discipline and time.

Most of us can't get away from our responsibilities long enough to ground this practice within us. When I say 'ground' I mean 'to take root,' so that it becomes so essential to our everyday life it becomes natural. The process starts by making a commitment to yourself. It is a way to start honoring and loving yourself that will have a positive effect on you, everyone you interact with and everything you do. It is the beginning of understanding the art of love.

Think about a time when you gave something your complete attention in order to perfect a skill. It probably took years to refine that skill. I'm sure it was a struggle at first, but the more you practiced the easier it became. The same will happen here, except you will also go deeper and deeper into your consciousness which will bring you great wisdom and help you to be the highest version of yourself. There's a great payoff to sticking with this, to keep coming back to it when you become distracted. The goal is to keep coming back home inside yourself.

Why don't you take a few moments right now to breathe and allow yourself to take in what you just read and to breathe out any anxiety or energy inside that is not serving you. Identify any thoughts or feelings that might be coming to the surface...observe them...feel them and then let go of them.

Write down what you experienced. This is important, especially if you have never had a meditative practice before. This book will help you to stop at times and become conscious of what is happening within you. I know you want to skip over this part and move on to the next chapter, but taking the time to be quiet and observe will enhance your awareness of all your previously unnoticed thoughts and feelings that are having tremendous affects upon you...many of which are negative.

Be patient with yourself. It takes time and practice. You will eventually get used to this process of feeling your feelings. In time you will easily be able to recognize your feelings as they emerge. The more you suppress your feelings, the more damage you do to your mind and body. You'll find that one of the benefits of this practice is that you will feel better, lighter, and have fewer aches and pains. You will be healthier due to all of the breathing exercises you are doing, and by working on being peaceful and calm.

Chapter Nine

Where Does All the Sickness Come From Anyway?

All sickness is projected from one's mind
Your soul is perfect and so are you
You never needed to be healed
Only from the belief that you are ill or broken

Many of our ailments, illnesses, and emotional stresses are a response to suppressed feelings. When we're flooding our mind with toxic negative thinking, fears and worries we're typically not recognizing and releasing our feelings which, in turn, are getting pushed back down into our body. Day after day this is happening. We keep swallowing all of the painful thoughts and feelings, and after a while, our body and mind can't take any more. There's no escape for all of this negative energy. This is one reason why many of us end up with so many physical, emotional and spiritual ailments.

As I walk this journey I look back at so many clients that had come into our clinical office for medication and/or therapy. I realize now that many of them were just experiencing symptoms of a Spiritual Awakening…a cry for love from within or their ego lambasting them and their soul trying to get them to heal their wounds. As an unhealed healer we miss all of these opportunities to help people in a very different way and truly makes me sad.

Deep breathing can minimize the devastating effects of negative energy. Just by breathing, you are changing your heart rate and the way your organs are working. You are letting go of tension from head to toe. You should also feel pain leave in different areas of your body just from relaxing with your breath. This is why meditation and yoga are excellent ways to teach you the importance of relaxation through deep breathing.

Let's discuss another benefit of deep breathing; it cleanses your mind. Your thought process will change to a more positive state and will begin to remove you from your ego-driven state of unconsciousness. Deep breathing is a built-in protection to help you recalibrate your thinking and to help you stay present.

You do have the power to heal yourself. This is very important as you travel through your life's journey. If you're hearing, witnessing, or feeling something that upsets you, just breathe through it. Once relaxation sets in and your mind has been cleared you have the opportunity to make a different choice in behavior, feeling, and thinking; you can hear your inner guidance and have an understanding of why you are getting affected by the event.

When you are present, you'll be amazed how different you feel in the moment. You will feel as though you have so much more control over yourself in a different way, a peaceful way. We all allow external events, people, places and things…including our ego and it's programming, to control us. The true meaning of being in control is to fully understand that you are quite capable of shutting out all of those disturbances and taking back your power. Isn't that what we all want anyway…to be in full control of ourselves and be free? Who would guess that all it takes is learning to recognize when to sit back and consciously take two or three deep breathes.

WHERE DOES ALL THE SICKNESS COME FROM ANYWAY?

Most of us have been trying to control our external world so that we feel esteemed, accepted, comfortable, safe and loved. We've all been trying to master how to do this, but it's really an impossible task, and there is no truth to any of it. Our external world does not supply us with self-esteem, love, or safety; they all come from within. None of us have been taught to master our internal world. Once you learn how to control your internal world, and the art of loving yourself, you will then have the ability to control your life and create the life that you dream about.

Shutting out the external world is difficult but it can be done even if only for short periods of time. When you quiet your mind you can recognize your ego's programming and start to see your truth…even if it's only for 10 – 15 minutes during your lunch break. Be by yourself and quiet the internal self-talk, the incessant chatter in your head. What you learn about yourself in those 10 – 15 minutes will be enormous. Maybe you can set your alarm clock 15 minutes earlier, or make time to go for a walk. If you need to do it when you go to bed, you can, but if you're tired and exhausted you'll have difficulty finding the necessary concentration and will fall asleep.

Most of us are exhausted trying to cram too much into each day, thinking too much, doing too much, not getting proper nutrition, sleep or exercise. Many say that they don't have time to take a break and practice being calm. But if you add up how much time you spend on Facebook, the internet, checking your emails, watching TV, getting lost in your thoughts, or some other distraction that has no real meaning, it will show you how much time is really available to you. Remember, nothing will rejuvenate you like a few minutes of meditative quiet time.

Imagine if you could find quiet time as a family and then have a few moments of individual time for yourself. You'd be giving your children a great gift and starting them on their way to mastering their own internal world. Parents are teachers. Your children will do what you role model to them, not necessarily what you tell them.

Why don't you stop right now and breathe. I want you to take a piece of paper or type out what behaviors you are role modeling to your children. If you don't have children, look at what you are role-modeling to others around you, your spouse, family, co-workers and friends. Ask yourself, how do others see me, not what are you trying to make them see. These are two very different things.

Most of us are presenting ourselves in either appearance (have to look a certain way) or performance (have to act or do things a certain way), or both, in an attempt to be viewed in a way that we think will garner approval, self-esteem, love and acceptance. This by the way is causing so much internal pressure, stress, and anxiety within that it's creating a chaotic internal environment that is hazardous to our health.

As we are doing this, we are unaware that we are also giving off other realities about ourselves. Are those realities positive, negative, anxious, tense, angry, fearful, or are they free and light? Do we appear frazzled, caught up in our busy-ness, with bags under our eyes from not sleeping well? Do we look like we're in a frenzy and are overwhelmed? And by the way, where is our heart in all of this; is it opened or closed? Do we take time for others and for our self? Are we irritable and snippy to our self and others? Do we do so much caretaking that we are not taking care of our self? Or, do we appear peaceful and loving in a light energetic flow? What is the energy that other people feel from you all day, at home, work, and play? When we take time to sit and breath we can begin to get answers to these questions and then ask ourselves whether we are happy with what we are role-modeling.

On March 25, 2016 I was having a discussion with Archangel Gabriel. My husband and I were in the process of selling our home and moving from Pennsylvania to Florida. I was also trying to establish a practice in Florida and just finished writing these books. I was feeling overwhelmed and was sick. Having become more aware of the stressful energy in my body I wanted it to stop and knew I needed to be replenished. Gabriel told me that I needed to allow the love and light to heal me and had me meditate for 1 ½ hours. He sat with me and guided me into the meditation by asking me to see the light of the sun as healing light nourishing my body and that I drink in his love and the light. After 1 ½ hours of this meditation I felt completely healed and nourished into a beautiful state of peace and love. This was my second understanding of how we have the ability to heal ourselves.

Archangel Gabriel's Meditation

Imagine yourself bathing in the ocean of your soul. Your soul is filled with unconditional love and beautiful white radiant light….and is much larger than your body…..Imagine a beautiful circle of white radiant light encapsulating you…..and allow it to heal you of everything you think needs to be healed within and without. Allow the light of God that embodies your soul to encompass you….Feel the light caressing every part of your body and mind…… See it move through your body as if you are invisible and the light is all you are made up of…..Beautiful pure white radiant light, God's light, divine light……Allow yourself to keep basking in the light as if the sun is radiating on you in a continuous stream….Breath in the light….and as you take breathes… allow the light to circulate all through your body….gently allowing the flow to move to every inch of your body....within and without.......Hold this image as long as you can....as you watch this light repair and regenerate every cell...and every organ from head to toe. Feel the beautiful warmth of the light as a loving energy...allowing every care in your mind to slip away......and all you feel is peace and love throughout your body.........Kissed by divine light, nurturing you back to your divine form......Breath in the light again and allow it to go into your lungs and fill every space within you. Feel your heart open with radiant love......and watch and feel the miracle of peace and love unfold within you....

You are blessed and loved beyond what you could ever imagine.....take that in with another breath of light.........Let any thoughts keep floating away....and focus on breathing in the light.....See it shimmering inside you........notice the stillness within and what your body and mind feel like at peace and complete rest........Continue to hold this meditation in your imagination as long as you need to......allowing it to continue on its own to heal you back to a divine state of being.

Chapter Ten

Beginning to See Your Truth

*The only truth about you
is that you are love & light
that you are a divine being
and dearly loved*

As you start to do this work, you'll begin to understand that who you have been and who you are, are completely different. The appearance you've been showing others is flawed. Most people can see through your outward presentation to what you're hiding from yourself…both the positives and the negatives. People will see gifts and strengths in you that are not in your own awareness. They will also see your shame, guilt, fear and low self-esteem.

Some of us have practiced our own personal appearance and performance for so long we can fool others as well as ourselves. This artfully constructed appearance is a product of our ego. Our ego is so bent on protecting us that it doesn't perceive any of our innate goodness, nor does it believe that we are capable of handling our life. So our ego constructs masks and invisible armor for us to wear on the outside in a desperate effort to hide what it sees as our weaknesses and vulnerabilities. But remember, what ego sees has no basis in truth.

The ego affects every area of our life. It creates misery and suffering when there is none. It thinks it can fix others when it has no control over others. It will take on unnecessary burdens of others to gain control and power over them in order to 'keep us safe, loved or to not feel guilty.' Our ego lives in denial and unreality.

The ego believes we're not safe, we're not strong enough and capable enough to survive in this world without its help; all of that is completely untrue. Maybe when you were younger you might not have been safe in the environment you were in. But if you are in an unsafe environment now, is it one of your own choosing? If you choose unsafe environments it is because you are projecting that is what you deserve or can expect from life due to an irrational belief that is part of your storyline that needs to be healed, such as, you are a victim. As an adult, we have power; as a child, we do not. Your ego can see your environment as being unsafe and will behave accordingly, but it's typically an illusion.

Look at the different areas of your life, relationships, home, work, finances, friends. What is it that you are perceiving that makes you feel unsafe? Take a few moments to write or type where you are fearful and what the truth is about that fear. Then I want you to look at how you behave in those areas when you are coming from a fearful place. You might start with what are you trying to control or have power over.

Let's start to breath again as you do this exercise. Did you find that you are projecting fear and then reacting or behaving in ways that you didn't recognize before? What patterns or energy are you seeing? Is this old energy? Could it be fear from when you were growing up and listening to your family speak about life events, people, finances, etc. Think about what you heard and learned that your ego has now incorporated into your programing. Can you see that you are listening to that programing and are reacting to the same old fears and thought patterns that were drilled into you or subtly influenced you as a child? Did your family see life as fearful and project that fear onto you? How about your grandparents or others you spent time with; what fears, anxieties, victimizations, entitlements, prejudices or irrational thoughts did they pass on to you? Fear is contagious just like every other feeling. If you are surrounded by fearful energy all the time, it becomes a part of you without you being aware of it, and most of the fear manifests as anxiety, then frustration and then anger.

How is fear keeping you from expressing your life differently? Is it holding you back from creating the life you truly want? What is it that your heart truly wants to do but you have been afraid? Remember, if we keep feeding the fear we'll give it more power. We need to overcome fear and become fearless in order to live a life of true happiness, fulfillment and purpose.

Since fear is part of being human and is all ego-driven, it is our life's journey to overcome it. Fear brings lack, anxiety, depression, scarcity, aloneness, anger and misery. We must keep pressing through and working on diminishing and eliminating the role of fear in our life.

It is normal to be scared as you're working through your fear. But you need to keep pushing through it until you have accomplished the goal you are working on. It's okay to feel fear but you can't let it stop you from what you are trying to achieve. We all look at fear as a weakness, but it's only a weakness when we give-in to it.

Fear can also be a great motivator…it all depends on the power you give it. Think of a time when you used fear to motivate you. What did you accomplish? Can you see the differences between what you are doing now that is inhibiting you as opposed to accelerating you? Being fearful means that you have no trust in yourself, others, or in God/Spirit.

As I started to do this work myself, I learned that I had a

lot of anxiety and did not recognize it. It was all based on my younger experiences and irrational fears of not performing up to expectations or being accepted, that I was not good enough and eventually someone would find out that I was a fraud, "the Imposter Syndrome!" These are very common misbeliefs by the way. I went through a period of time then of noticing all the anxiety that I was detached from by staying very busy with work. As a teenager, I had learned to suppress the anxiety from the trauma I experienced so not to show any vulnerability, and I continued to do it throughout my life. It was a huge eye opener when I finally came to understand what was really going on inside me. That understanding allowed me to start to address the fears that kept me trapped in my smallness, my ego.

Journal Entry 12/24/2015
With God

Me: *I have been thinking about my misconceptions from experiences/ programing and what I have learned growing up. I am causing all of my own trauma in my mind by believing things I shouldn't, such as, I am not safe, I am a victim, I am not good enough, no one is there for me, I can't trust anyone or myself, I am a disappointment, I am a fraud, I have to work hard to get ahead or to get people to like or love me, I have to be a good girl and make other people happy, I am not enough, I am unworthy, I can't be alone, I can't be vulnerable, I am shameful, I am guilty, I am not liked or loved. I can go on and on.* **God:** *What are you going to do with all of this programing?*

Me: *I am not sure what to do except stop listening or believing it.*
God: *Just observe and let go when you hear these things, do not react to it.* ***Me:*** *Is there anything else I can do? Just let it go, be mindful that this is a tape playing in my head? This is so hard to do.* ***God:*** *You get stuck in you own mind. It happens when you are not present. It is nothing to hold onto anymore. You are not a victim anymore. No one is victimizing you, but you. It is a bad habit that will take time to erase. Go about your life in grace with no worries. You do not need to defend yourself, let go of the protective armor. You do not have to prove yourself to anyone by consistently telling people what you've learned. Just 'Be' until asked.*

I wanted to share what I was learning, seeing and hearing with everyone so badly. I was exploding with light and love. I felt like the little kid who just got a great prize in the crackerjack box or someone who just hit the lottery! Hey, do you know what is inside each of us? We have access to God's love directly and a spiritual realm that helps us understand who we truly are and heals us! And guess what, we don't really die! I also recognized that this was also a pattern I had to try to receive validation from others. Being human is fascinating to me, I had God validating me and yet I still needed more validation.

Chapter Eleven

Faith versus Trust

*There is no greater joy
than to learn you have nothing to fear
Everything is planned & perfect
Trust in the only one who knows your heart*

Let's look a little deeper into the difference between faith and trust. We say we have faith in God/Spirit but there is no trust. You can't have one without the other; they go hand in hand. Many of us believe we trust, but if you break down thoughts and feelings during the day you will see how little we really trust anything.

Carefully examine your behaviors. Are you acting in a peaceful calm way as though your life is perfectly fine the way it is and you have nothing to worry about? Or, are you worried, sad and feel like you need to keep doing more or better in order to attain the goal of contentment within and without? This is fear. Do you trust that the people in your life are there to help you? Do you feel like you're living this life alone in a rat race to get to the next thing? Do you live with fear as a guiding presence in your life? If so, you don't trust yourself, God/Spirit, or anyone else.

How do we develop trust? How do we erase all of our programing about trust that we have learned? We have to go back to our initial soul/spirit's first truth because it is the only truth. We have all learned or assumed that others are responsible for our feelings, happiness and well being because this was our experience throughout the early stages of our life. It's now entrenched into our wounded adult ego programing. Many of us have also learned that we are responsible for other's feelings, happiness and well-being.

There is no truth to either of these. We are talking about adulthood, not raising children. We continue to get let down because of these irrational expectations or we burn ourselves out trying to care-take and make others happy by taking care of their responsibilities. Along the way we get angry and disappointed because we are not getting our needs met. If we do this, we always come up empty or disappointed. If these are familiar patterns in your life then they are part of the lessons you are here to learn and they will continue to reoccur until you go within and heal them.

We blame others for our emptiness, loneliness, heartache, exhaustion, grief, anger or whatever pain we are experiencing. We do this because we do not know how to take care of or process our own feelings, nor do we understand that we are responsible for the way we feel.

This is tricky because in some situations it could very easily appear as though someone hurt you tremendously and they might not have lived up to your expectations, but they do not make you feel. We alone choose how we want to feel…happy, sad, angry, etc.; we alone also choose the intensity of our feelings. Because so many of us have not been taught how to take responsibility for our feelings, we can feel as though we're on an emotional roller coaster allowing every thought, person, event to take us on a wild ride throughout the day. Or sometimes we are just numb and don't care. We become passive and apathetic, or maybe we are so detached from our emotions that we don't even know what's going on inside. This is where deep breathing is important.

It is your job to recognize the thoughts, feelings and energy inside you and to defuse negativity with deep breathing as you process your feelings, rather than expose or project it onto others. Once you can defuse the energy (not suppress it) you can look at what's causing it. Ninety-nine percent of the time that negative energy is coming from you.

As you go inside and begin to take responsibility for your own feelings you will start to develop trust in your ability to handle any situation. You will no longer give your power away to others. You will realize that you are not helpless. As you become stronger inside, you'll be able to connect more to yourself, God/Spirit. This takes time to practice as well. We are still on our journey. The faith and trust will start to come into greater alignment with God/Spirit when we stop looking outside our self to feel fulfilled. Your guidance and your soul will always nurture and love you; you'll start learning the art of love. You'll find that you now appreciate others more since you are no longer needy for them. We now simply want to love them.

When you can truly understand that other people are not there to make you feel safe and happy, they are not obligated to keep you content, entertained, comfortable or fill your love tank, you will have achieved a fantastic shift in your growth. When we can stop trying to manage other people's lives, behaviors and emotions, we feel better inside. Once this internal mastery and understanding comes together for you it will change all of your relationships to be more loving, or you will remove yourself from those relationships that are destructive and unhealthy. These are huge steps to take, but it is your responsibility to take them. No one is responsible for you but you.

My first awakening to this was when I read one of Margaret Paul's articles in the Huffington Post. She talked about how we cause ourselves pain by not taking responsibility for our own feelings and described four ways in which we self-abandon and do self rejecting behaviors. To sum them up they were;

First, we are judging ourselves harshly which causes us shame and guilt, which she states is easier for us to feel then dealing with the painful feelings in our life or heart. We believe that judging ourselves will give us control to get us to do things right, believing that if we could just get things right then someone will love us and give us the love that we are not giving to ourselves.

Second, we stay stuck in our head rather than being present in our body.

Third, we turn to addictions to numb ourselves.

Fourth, we blame others for the way we feel.

When I read this, my veil started to lift, the light bulbs started to go on for me. Hey, I do these things and it was not in my awareness. Although, I knew I was responsible for how I felt, I was not applying it nor did I know how to take responsibility for my own feelings with compassion and love. I found it easier to give compassion to others than myself; it is something I continue to work on to this day.

FAITH VERSUS TRUST

Journal entry 11/15/2015
A visual meditation with God

God and I are floating in the ocean on our backs. He has his arm around the back of my neck so I can rest on him and keep me afloat on the water peacefully while there is tension in the water, sharks, whales, fish swimming around us but I know I am safe floating with him. As we continue the water is filled with turbulence, it feels like anger, frenzy and appears to be unsafe. Fear, anxiety and unsafe feelings arise within me but I am trusting that I am fine being in God's arms. We are floating away from land, I not knowing the direction we are going but continue to float out to sea. I am feeling more secure with Him, it doesn't matter where we are going and that I cannot see the future or the path that gets me from A to B. I keep believing and leaning on his steadiness, I cannot get this from anyone else although I have tried my whole life. He brings me peace. **God:** *Look how you just calmed yourself down.* **Me:** *Thank you, but it came from being with you.* **God:** *Yes but you allowed the flow of my love into you and then it moved all of the negative energy out.*

Chapter Twelve

Mind Blowing

What will it take for you to believe me?
Don't take my word for it
Come, see it for yourself
See the treasure that awaits within you

I know this is a lot to take in. But when you experience it for yourself you will start to understand. This is nothing like any drug or high can give you; and by the way, if you are using any drugs or alcohol and try to do this, it won't work. Anything that creates an altered state of mind will impede your ability to look inward and find your truth. Narcotics, benzodiazepines and sedative medications will also impede this process since they put you in an altered, unconscious state when you are using them; they are basically numbing agents.

Sometimes we like being numb and unconscious rather than taking responsibility for fixing ourselves, healing ourselves and discovering the real truth of our lives. Truth is, there's no better high than being conscious, present, connected to Spirit and living with passion and purpose.

I encourage you to look at what you are doing to numb yourself, not just with drugs and alcohol, so we can work through these addictions. You deserve more than what you are giving or doing to yourself.

It is easy to look at life as 'it is what it is', accepting less than we deserve. We tend to punish ourselves rather than go inside to attain enlightenment and understanding. This is no one's fault. It is simply a lack of awareness and understanding. We have not been taught or shown how to do this. Our ego is more than happy to indulge us in everything and anything that keeps us from going inside and connecting to our Spirit. Our ego does not believe in Spirit or trust that we can get anything useful from inside. The truth is that when we find our inner guidance we start receiving all of the reassurance, love, peace and contentment that we need. Our ego is no longer needed. As it loses its power it fights to retain its control over you.

The ego wants to reassure us that it is protecting us however, in reality, it is simply giving more power to all of our negative programming. This is how habits and addictive behavior starts.

Let's just look at 'comfort food.' Say, you are having a bad day and you find yourself wanting to distract yourself from your feelings but you're really unconscious of this so you might choose to eat foods that are high in sugar, carbohydrates or maybe some chocolates. Can you hear your little inner child saying "Yum… I'm going to eat whatever I want and no one is going to tell me what to do, even if I have to sneak it?" You'll eat it and it might feel good to indulge at first, filling the emptiness or bad feelings inside you as they get buried under the food.

But then you begin to metabolize what you just ate and the sugar turns into lethargy and now you're tired, exhausted and feeling guilty and ashamed. At times I felt intoxicated by the food I was eating, I called it "drunk with food." You had a momentary release, a momentary high, but then you come down hard and fast. You get addicted to this cycle just so you don't have to deal with your painful feelings and emotions. Alcohol, smoking, drugs, shopping, exercise, gambling, socializing, care-taking, internet, too much TV, etc. It's all the same habitual cycle and it forces us to repeat the patterns over and over again just to avoid real or perceived pain. We make life so much more complicated than it needs to be and this is all self-rejecting and self-abandoning behavior.

Imagine what it would be like if you could just connect spiritually to your guidance/soul/spirit, sit and talk about what is bothering you, understand the truth about it, process it, feel it and let it go without having to harm yourself with these destructive cycles. This needs to become a habit in order to override the programing and allow you to break the repetitive cycles you are currently involved in. The more you practice being quiet, meditating, breathing, and connecting, one by one each of the old programs and patterns and energy will defuse and drop away over time. You will see that they no longer serve you and you won't want to be their prisoner anymore.

You have the power to heal yourself of all of these things. As you keep practicing you gain the insight that you want more from life and deserve more than you have been giving yourself or trying to get from others. Your ego is creating all of the pain you feel in order to distract you from the pain within that has been unhealed.

Once I started to work with each one of my wounded selves, (and there are many, starting at age 5) many of the patterns and energies dissipated, although the process of mastering myself still continues.

Chapter Thirteen

We Are All Self-Sufficient

In the space of time that you are allotted on earth
many events will arise that allow you to work through karmic lessons
They are all designed to grow your consciousness
Nothing is really happening to you it is all an illusion
You are always safe

No one ever told us we are self-sufficient. We have been given everything within us that we will ever need…all of the abilities, creativity, wisdom, knowledge, love, safety, passion, and joy. When we recognize that it is our journey to learn how to open our heart to our self, then our heart and mind can be filled with all of the greatness within us. Our job then becomes to share our love and light with others, engage in our own unique creativity, and use it as our vehicle for sharing. These books are my vehicle to share with you what I have learned as I've traveled along the path of my own personal journey so far.

We don't believe we are self-sufficient; we don't believe we are 'enough or worthy.' Therefore, we are constantly looking outside of our self to fill this empty void of aloneness, unworthiness and reassurance. All of these feelings come from the suffering of being separated from our soul/God/Spirit. This is self-defeating and self-abandoning. Others will never be able to fill the void, or the empty love tank we feel within us or give us self-esteem. If you think that someone or some thing is making you happy, it is a false sense of security. There is no joy like understanding that you create your own happiness. This is very powerful, especially when you come to realize that no one can ever take that power away from you either. You decide whether you want to be happy or not. You have the ability to connect yourself to happiness and gratitude every day and every moment of the day. Your happiness does not depend on your location, events, people or things.

If you become aware that you are feeling unhappy, all you need to do is take a few breaths and set your intensions to be happy and identify what you are grateful for. It will bring a peace and contentment to your whole being.

We make decisions unconsciously every moment of the day regarding how we want to feel. We have been used to operating at the feeling state or vibration that was set a long time ago, and our mind and body are used to being in that state; it becomes a habit. We need to change our feeling set point just like we have to do with our weight. If you have ever been on a diet then you probably experienced that as soon as you stop managing your diet and exercise your body tends to return to the weight at which your body feels comfortable…your set point.

Many times, our feeling state is tied into that body weight set point. For example, if you are feeling overwhelmed or sad or depressed and your addiction to numb yourself is to eat more, you are going to establish a set point weight that matches your mood. These are cycles that we go through.

It is the same if we are experiencing physical pain. Our mind/mood tries to get in alignment with that pain. When you see this, you recognize how important it is to keep your attitude positive and to keep recalibrating your emotional state to happiness and gratitude. If you can master this art of recalibrating, you'll find that you have less pain in your body.

Let's take a moment to take some deep breaths and notice what it is that you're feeling right now. What sensations do you have in your body? Do you feel light or heavy, tense or loose? Is your breathing labored or easy? Now think about your day or even the last couple of hours. What has your attitude been? What have you been feeling and thinking? Have you been positive or negative? It's crucial to gain understanding of all of this for you are not just affecting yourself you're affecting everyone and everything that comes into your path. Wherever you go, this energy will follow you.

Chapter Fourteen

This Energy Will Follow You

*Please hold onto the love that is yours
it is your divine right. Never let go of it
for it is your pathway to enlightenment*

The energy inside of us also affects others. Understanding how you are feeling will also allow you to know how other people are 'feeling' you. When I started to do this work, I realized that as my children were growing up they had been feeling and sensing everything I was trying to hide from myself. We try very hard to hide our emotions, especially if they are negative, but we are constantly transmitting this energy whether we want to or not. We are reading everyone's energy or 'vibe', and they are reading ours; it happens naturally and unconsciously. When we notice something unusual in someone's energy we become aware of it consciously. You can see why it's important to understand the energy you are transmitting, especially since you may be sending a message you don't want to convey.

Think about how hard we work to hide our feelings, especially at work. Everyone is trying to be on her/his best behavior, well sometimes, LOL. This takes an enormous amount of energy and causes a lot of tension and anxiety. When we return home from work, most of us are more relaxed and are not on guard quite as much, however, we can be exhausted from controlling ourselves all day. Some of us feel very tense at home too, imagine what all of this is doing to us on a cellular level, our body and mind are constantly taking hits. What energy is your family feeling from you? We touched on this in the last chapter, but now you know that you are capable of changing that energy to radiate more positively.

Many of us put so much emphasis on performance, especially at work, but we don't apply the same emphasis and effort at home. We act as though one area of our life is more important than another. We can also be exhausted from controlling and performing all day at work that we lose it when we come home or just shut down. Do you put the same energy into taking care of yourself? That is an interesting question because, as you now see, it takes more than just eating well and exercising to maintain one's physical, emotional and spiritual health.

Most of us take for granted our mood/emotional state/attitude, our heart. This is crucial to our own quality of life and to the quality of life we offer those around us. Once you begin to be able to quiet your mind, explore your inner self and access your guidance you'll begin to have a positive effect on everyone around you; and it happens very quickly. You won't even have to tell anyone what you are doing. They will see dramatic changes in you, especially in your energy. You'll appear happier, more relaxed and loving. How lucky they will be that you are doing this work! It will shift the energy in others automatically because their energy will want to be in harmony with yours.

If this happens on a small scale, imagine what happens on a larger scale if many people are doing this work simultaneously. There can be much more harmony within our families, our communities, and in our world. In fact, that's one of the purposes of this book, to show people a way of attaining self-enlightenment and heightened awareness in order to create a harmonious shift in the world. Just you, one person, can have a dramatic affect on many people. Those people can and will have dramatic affects on others and so on.

Look at the work you are doing as your part in attaining world peace. It's a blessing to yourself and to so many others. We have so much power to make change…and it all starts with us individually. We have the ability to affect so many people in a single day just by sharing the love we have found within ourselves. This is all it takes, sharing love.

Sounds easy, doesn't it? It isn't. The process of opening your heart and keeping it open is a journey. If you are reading this book, then you are ready and have already started down this path. You know you are being called to do more and to be more than you have been. There is greatness inside of you and it is your journey to find it. Ultimately, what you find has always been there waiting for you. There is no time like the present, and the clock is ticking. Each time you delay starting your journey you waste precious time. For as we all know, our time here on earth is limited.

Journal Entry 10/31/2015
With Jesus

Me: *I have been learning through my University class and from Barbara about how energy is transmitted generationally. I guess we need to be responsible for the energy we put out there.* **Jesus:** *Yes, and consider that most people do not know this. It is a huge challenge for* most people to understand. **Me:** *We need to communicate our feelings appropriately, not acting on them to discharge the energy but what else is there, say you are alone? Does journaling, praying, deep breathing discharge it so you are not polluting the planet?* **Jesus:** *That is an excellent question. Well, you have seen that journaling and talking with and loving your wounded selves through guided imagery transforms that negative energy into love and peace.* **Me:** *I see. Then you are not polluting the air by venting it on yourself or someone else.* **Jesus:** *Yes. You do it by loving yourself, and if prayer, meditation, yoga, or anything else helps you to go inside yourself to find the problem and then confront it and love it, that will help change the energy also. Then, if you need to talk to someone about it, the energy has already changed and they will be more receptive to talk.*

Chapter Fifteen

It's Crunch Time

*"Blessed is thou who wants to take the time to seek within
To do the work of the angels
Spread your wings and fly with me to healing"*

You will have to have a lot of patience, honesty and perseverance to do this work. You'll encounter many bumps along the road and will keep running into your ego that has a completely separate agenda. The bumps will be erected by what you may have heard called your 'shadow side', ego, or wounded selves…the parts of you that you keep hidden, even from yourself.

All the pain that has been suppressed and repressed will keep creating events in your life and come up to greet you. This can also be looked at as all of the Karmic lessons you need to overcome and heal. All of your weaknesses and parts of yourself that you are uncomfortable with will now be in your awareness. Don't run from them. Breathe, observe and understand where they come from. Your ego will taunt you with all of these 'weaknesses'; it will scrutinize your entire humanity. I go into more depth about this in the next volume. It is our job to embrace all of our different facets, the traits we would consider weaknesses and strengths and not judge them. We are perfect just the way we are. It is our patterns and beliefs that need to be corrected.

We have all heard of internal battles, the fight between good and evil, etc. This is what the process feels like. As you keep digging and not judging yourself, so much more will be revealed to you. Your ego will become more and more desperate since it knows it is losing control over you. Your ego will make you feel bad so it can keep its hooks in you. Remember, ego is only doing this to protect you because it does not understand why you are turning away from listening to it.

At times you'll feel like you are fighting for your life, and you are, you are fighting for your freedom. This can have some real physical effects on you. You may feel as though you've lost your balance, your physical and emotional equilibrium. The energy within you will increase and at times you will feel as though you are about to explode with fear, anxiety, frustration or anger. Keep breathing and use your meditation/relaxation skills. Make sure that you are keeping yourself physically active. Activities like walking, dancing, jogging provide important ways to deal with the excess internal energy that you may experience.

Journal what you find happening within you. Think of it as though you are experiencing symptoms of a spiritual awakening. It is a battle of wills, you and your ego and all the feelings you have been suppressing coming up at once as energy, including the spiritual energy of your soul. Your soul is pushing everything up at the same time for you to heal it. It's saying 'Come on, let's do this already, we have lots of creating to do!'

I don't mean to scare you, but understanding the nature of what is happening within you will be very helpful. Most of all, know that you can do this! Think of it as rebirthing yourself. Think about how a baby must feel in the womb as it grows and doesn't have enough room to straighten out anymore. It's an intensely frustrating time and you need to take extra care of yourself during this rebirthing process. And, by the way, we go through these stages of spiritual symptoms several times as we expand our consciousness. Keep breathing through it.

You're probably thinking, why would anyone want to do this? Well, it is the reason we are here, to dig down within until we find our highest. This is how we make meaning and purpose of our life. It is how we return to our soul/spirit to be one with God/Spirit. It will get easier over time, and the terrible discomfort will dissipate as you grow and become more in line with your soul/spirit than with your ego.

It's really a fascinating process and you will be in awe of what you witness, accomplish and learn. What a joy to watch and witness as your heart gradually opens and becomes filled with love, grace, and compassion. You will like your new self. You will be ready to release all of your former pain, shame, guilt, anger, blame, aloneness, resentments, grief, loss and despair. I believe it is worth all of the hard work, and so will you. You will embrace your humanity, even your ego, and understand that it is a gift to have this opportunity to experience a new purposeful life; you will be grateful.

This can be a difficult process emotionally and it is crucial for you to be connected to your spiritual guidance to aid you, love you, and help you understand the process you are going through. As I kept digging deeper through meditation and journaling I uncovered all of my pain, anger, delusional thoughts about myself and others. I felt completely raw, vulnerable and exposed. The patterns of shame, guilt and unworthiness that came to light were overwhelming. I had kept much of the shame, guilt and unworthiness hidden away in my shadow side so when I came face to face with the depth of these feelings it was shocking. I had no idea of the strength and depth of these feelings until I did this work.

All human beings carry some degree of shame, guilt and unworthiness unknowingly, unconsciously. In the journal entry after Chapter 4 you can see how I was projecting the belief of unworthiness onto God. I had also projected this onto my Spiritual guides, however, God and my guides loved me through it and helped me assess what is true and what is not true about myself. There is no hierarchy between us and God. I AM God. You are God. We all are God.

The feelings of shame, guilt and unworthiness arose from the deeply layered generational programming that all of us inherit as humans, and from my experiences, family and society. It's the same for all of us. The unconditional love and Spiritual Re-parenting that I experienced allowed me to heal the pain of these beliefs and forgive myself and others for what I or they had done wrong. Because we believe such terrible things about our self and others we have judgmental thoughts and behavioral patterns that create more conflict both internally and externally. Our thoughts and patterns set us up to think and act in ways that are not in our highest. We do all of this unknowingly or with minimal awareness because the thoughts and patterns become ingrained as our natural/normal behavior. It was, and is, a very messy process. My passion to be healed was much more important than the messiness or the process, so I kept digging. This type of healing can only be done through God/Spirit; traditional therapy does not lead to this depth of healing especially when we are unhealed healers like I had been. It's easy to keep looking outside for an understanding of what you are going through rather than turning inside to our spiritual guidance and asking for help and support. I know first hand as I am still looking for explanations outside even knowing what I already have inside, it is part of the spiritual process. It is still the ego not wanting to accept what is.

However, it is also comforting to know that other seekers are going through the same kind of process and experiencing the same kinds of things as you are. It also helps to know and learn from others who have walked this path. Something important to remember is that each person's journey will be different since they have their own Spiritual path and instruction. We can't simply follow someone else's path. Your Spiritual compass is inside of you and it is unique to each person. Your guidance is there to help you understand you. All the answers are within you and part of your journey is to learn how to trust yourself and guidance/Spirit more than anything else in the world. You are the only one that knows what is best for you and what you need.

Chapter Sixteen

So What Does All of This Mean?

Peace comes to the one who seeks
There is solace in knowing who you truly are
It brings freedom to the courageous
for they are the true fighters for love

It means that we are the creator of our own lives. Whatever you believe, think or feel gives power to your creation, consciously and unconsciously. Our spirit knows we are here to learn a series of spiritual lessons and evolve. As the creator of our own life, we prearranged a life that we think will teach us the lessons that we need to learn in order to attain a higher level of spiritual consciousness.

The problem is that we've lost contact with our soul's first truth; we've become unconscious. We're creating our current life from our unconscious mind, our ego mind, which is simply a collection of stories that we assume about ourselves and others. As a result, we create lives filled with a succession of painful events… over, and over, and over again. We make life stressful because our unconscious mind believes we need to suffer. It is the addiction cycle again. Our mind and body get used to the painful events and we become programed to think that the pain and stress is normal, or it's just our life. But it isn't 'just our life,' we're simply not getting it. We're not seeing that we need to wake up and ask internally why and what is my life about? What am I doing that caused this pain? Why do I feel so stuck and why can't I ever seem to figure out what needs to be changed?

Understanding and accepting that this is true is just one level of consciousness; and I will tell you that it takes both time and hard work to reach and assimilate this level of understanding. Our ego, of course, believes that this scenario is a lie since it fears losing control once you understand and accept the truth. Your ego will resist your accepting the truth, but much of the awakening is transcending the ego. Have patience with this; have patience with yourself; it's a lot to absorb. I still wrestle with this at times.

Clarity will come if you continue working on this path. So let's take some paper out and look at what your programming and your ego is telling you about what you just read. Be honest about all the feelings that come up and don't judge them.

Breathe, and continue to take deep breaths. Relax, and when you feel centered, ask your soul/spirit or your guidance the truth about what you are reading. Write down anything you hear or know through your heart. Keep breathing deep breaths…in through your nose and out through your mouth. Center your focus into your heart as you breath imagining that your heart is growing bigger and bigger and opening at the same time. The more that you invite love and light in and want to know your truth, the more answers you will receive. Knowing your truth is being loving to yourself. Don't be afraid of what you will hear, for it is always loving and honest. Your guidance/soul/spirit is not going to give you more than what you are ready for.

At times, depending on the frame of mind or mood you're in, it can take quite a while of breathing into your heart to get your consciousness to expand enough to move your ego out of the way. This is normal. Just keep practicing. Remember, you are also healing yourself while you do deep breathing, so it's good for you on multiple levels. Pace your deep breaths so you are not taking them too close together; you don't want to hyperventilate!

Find your natural breathing rhythm, count five or ten seconds and take another deep breath. It's like cleaning the cobwebs out of your mind and body. "Ahh… all is well." This is a very useful mantra to use anytime you might feel a struggle within yourself. "All is well; everything is as it should be." A friend of mine Mari-Etta Stoner uses "Everything is working perfectly", it too is a wonderful mantra.

If you look at every emotional conflict that arises in you as having a purpose of getting your attention to try to be healed, and if you dig to understand the truth about that conflict, it will make the healing process much easier. Understand that each feeling, each conflict, is built upon multiple layers of thoughts, feelings and behaviors from experiences. If you observe your thoughts and feelings rather than reacting to them, you can begin to follow the thread of those thoughts and feelings back to their origination point, which may go all the way back deep into your childhood; most do.

It is possible to heal the conflicts both within you and outside of you with love. You do this by understanding the nature of the conflicts and accepting that each conflict presents an opportunity to wake up and become present and conscious. By avoiding, suppressing or blaming others for our feelings we are simply continuing to give in to our ego, which will inevitably lead to even more conflict. Embrace your feelings and emotions. Embrace them as opportunities for personal growth and spiritual awakening.

Chapter Seventeen

Consciously Creating

Allow me to witness the unfolding of the beauty within you
I have left it there as a treasure for you to find
Nothing makes me happier then
seeing you shimmer in your divinity

If we are awake, present and conscious, and understand that life is an illusion of our creation, then we can change our lives completely by giving power to thoughts of love, goodwill and creating purpose and beauty.

As you continue to work with your spirit and dig for your gifts, talents and expression of love, your spirit and the universe will align with you to create the life you were meant to have. Your purpose is to be love and joy. When you are finally able to express your gifts of love and light, your life will become one of abundance, peace, tranquility, love and harmony, especially internally. It doesn't mean however, that we will never have to deal with difficult events.

We all express our gifts differently. As spirit, we are all the same love and light. As human beings, we have different personalities and talents that are unique to us. Whether it be through music, art, writing, speaking, healing, or being the best parent or employee you can be, there are so many ways for us to express our love and light and bring joy to others and ourselves.

Remember, just by becoming awake, opening your heart, and increasing your positive energy, you impact others on a profound level. You are here to create. Now that you understand that the life you have been living is simply a dream, an illusion, you can change your dream/story going forward to bring yourself into alignment with your understanding of your true purpose and your unique expression in life. It is easy to get cynical about all this, but that's just your ego trying to divert you in order to maintain its control. Don't be distracted. You have felt so much pain. Your pain has been real to you, and it has affected your life. Realize that everyone around you has also felt her/his own pain. Understand that they are still hurting and are struggling to awaken from their story, their dream. It is important to show compassion and grace for yourself and for others.

You now have the chance to let your spirit shine through and accept your humanity. You have a chance to be in your highest form and to come into the person you were meant to be…pure love and light to express and share your talents with others so they can be inspired.

You just need to be you. You don't need to talk others into waking up; it typically doesn't work. We all have our own awakening date. Each person, along with God/Spirit sets that date and each person who awakes is woken up at the perfect time.

When you wake up and start to see truth it's very exciting and you'll want to share it, but most people won't be ready to receive it. Living awake can be lonely at times if your family and friends don't understand. You have to keep going into yourself and discuss all of this with your guidance/Spirit. It is part of your learning process to get all of your recognition, reassurance, love, friendship, trust and self-esteem from within you. It strengthens who you are so you can then share yourself with others from your highest and not your ego.

It's all part of the journey. The truth about you and about everything around you is found within. At some point soon, your gifts will appear and you will grace others with those gifts. People may ask 'how did you do this?' 'How do I get to that same place of peace, love, and abundant gifts?' This, then, is your opportunity to speak your truth…when you have an eager ear ready to listen. Otherwise you may become very disappointed when no one else shares your newfound awareness. I know I wanted to shout it to everyone. I tried but many did not understand and were not interested or ready to listen.

If you were to create a new life or story, what would it look like? Having a vision is critical to manifesting it. You can't build what you can't envision. If you are struggling with seeing your vision, ask your guidance/Spirit to help you during your meditations. Remember, this is a work in progress and it will affect many different areas of your life…individually, spiritually, physically, and emotionally. It will affect your family, your career, and how you are going to serve others with your love, light and gifts.

Take out a piece of paper and just start random writing. Start from a standpoint of not having to worry about finances, or time, so your fears don't hold you back. Create as big a vision as you can without fear, hesitation, or judgment from your ego. Let go and create the life that you think will be the most fulfilling for you. There is no right or wrong. Write down anything that pops into your mind that you wish to have or want, even specific skills… write them down. If you can't envision what your talent or gifts are then start with what you would be feeling if you have already achieved this wonderful life. What would your life look like, how would you feel? Work backwards. It's like reverse engineering (You might want to explore the program by Derek Rydall – Soul Purpose Blueprint.)

Never stop dreaming, for dreams do come true. After all,

you are the creator of your own destiny. I am living mine! God bless you.

Journal Entry 10/21/15
Discussion with Jesus continued:

Me: Sometimes I read about people who have awakened and it appears as if they look at life as if it is a big game. **Jesus:** *I know some people are still missing the significance when they awaken. This is the Spiritual Ego. Please do not look at this as a game: that is the wrong intention, although it does not mean you cannot have fun.* **Me:** *I am being told that I can create and manifest whatever I want.* **Jesus:** *Well you can and you have been doing it all along, but it cannot be with a feel of disingenuousness, as if it is a big joke on everyone. You know you are powerful already.* **Me:** *How do I funnel this so that I can move into my gifts?* **Jesus:** *You need to remain calm and peaceful and trusting of God to bring you to each phase as you are ready for it. You need to harness your exhilaration and your wanting to let this energy race in you. Your power is in your peace and tranquility. Knowing that you are blessed and that everything you need and want is being brought to you so you can enjoy your life with gratitude and you do not have to worry. The peace within you is what draws people to you.* **Me:** *How do I harness this energy into a sense of peace and calmness?* **Jesus:** *I know this sounds hard but it is not. Can you see the energy as just vibration and allow your self to just vibrate it and not have to do something with it.* **Me:** *I guess that makes sense.* **Jesus:** *You will get used to having the vibration of spiritual energy. It means you are alive* *inside.* **Me:** *So I can be calm within the energy?* **Jesus:** *Yes, it does not have to be discharged. Just resonate in it, and let it flow through you, deep breathe it out if you need to. It is God's love. It is like singing a song to you, a beautiful, energetic melody of love and aliveness.*

I asked these questions due to the exhilaration I was feeling and felt like I needed to do something with the energy, like run or jump around, move in some way or shop! I was not used to being still and calm with it. Spiritual energy feels like tingling all through your body. It is like having goose bumps on the inside!

About the Author

Debbie N. Goldberg practiced as a clinical therapist for 18 years in Pennsylvania specializing in mental health and substance abuse issues for adults and couples. She has worked in a variety of settings and is now in private practice as a Spiritual Mentor residing in Islamorada, Florida. She brings the spiritual knowledge of her own awakening into her work to inspire healing, love, joy, purpose and creativity as each of us works through our own spiritual journey.

Acknowledgements

There are several people and spiritual guides that I want to thank. If it were not for all of you, I would not have evolved to this place of knowingness and love. My life has been filled with such grace and blessings and I want to honor everyone.

I thank God and Jesus for their never-ending unconditional love, spiritual re-parenting and for showing me the path, purpose and freedom that awaits me. Thank you for healing and restoring me and teaching me what love truly is. The love that comes from spirit is transformative love and teaches you the art of love, of loving yourself and others. I am so grateful and honored to have you walking beside me as I navigate the rest of my life.

My highest and all of my other divine spiritual guides who role model what and who a more loving me is.

My husband whose patience, love, nurturing and support gives me the courage to follow my heart and holds me up when I fall down, who believes in me and walks this path of spiritual growth with me. I am eternally grateful for his typing and editing of these books. It has been an honor to be your wife; you are a beautiful human being and a blessing to my life. I love you…

My parents, children and family who play such a role of love and grace in my life, I love you. We have all struggled together and apart and amongst each other throughout life, all becoming better because of it. You are the catalyst to make me try harder to be a blessing rather than a burden and to transform all of the negative generational transmissions that we share.

To all of my friends who have supported me and to all of my

enemies who have sought to diminish me, your combined energies have pushed me to want to be my highest. I love you.

A very special thank you to everyone who helped with editing and input for these books, Michelle Beber, Mari-Etta Stoner -http://www.everythingisworkingperfectly.com, and Lois Huling. All of your special touches helped in this creation.

To Dr. Barbara De Angelis, and to all the members of her 'Vortex.' Your work has accelerated my growth in consciousness, love, and compassion for myself and others. Barbara is a road map of love and light in navigating our complex world of the ego and transcending into our highest self. These books are sprinkled with the love and wisdom that I have received from you as well. I hope they will play some small part in continuing to spread that same love and wisdom to others.

To Dr. Margaret Paul and Dr. Erica Chopich. Thank you for your divine gift of 'Inner Bonding' and your beautiful guided imagery tools. These have been the most healing techniques I have shared with my wonderful clients and myself. I am forever grateful for they have allowed me to connect spiritually through sight, hearing and knowingness. They have changed my life in understanding myself and seeing that I am not alone, that God, Jesus, and Spirit walk with me, and that I have a higher self within me. They have allowed me to channel these books and blend the lessons with Jesus and your teachings. They have brought me to my purpose.

To Joel Osteen. You are a divine being of love that spreads light and hope to everyone. I look forward to your seminars every Sunday morning. They are blessings that lift me up and help me to stay lifted. Your words are blended into these books. Thank you for your devotion in spreading God's love.

To Boni Lonnsburry, author of 'The Map and Living a Life Worth Living.' Thank you Boni for your map of conscious creating and understanding the Law of Attraction. It has allowed me to consciously create a life worth living.

To Derek Rydall author of Soul Purpose Blueprint and Emergineering. Thank you for these amazing programs that allowed me to open up to the opportunity of finding my purpose and what was blocking me. It is an excellent program.

To Nick Peters LMT, Massage and Myofascial Therapist. I started receiving massage therapy from Nick at the beginning of my spiritual awakening. At the time, I had a lot of muscular pain in different parts of my body. Through the fifteen months of treatment I learned a lot about how emotional pain and negative energy is stored in the body. Nick helped me to move that energy out. Physically and emotionally I now feel like a new human being. I honor his healing techniques.

A very honorable mention and thank you to Dr. Jason E. Gines, Assistant Professor of Education (Counselor Education & Rehabilitation and Human Services) at The Pennsylvania State University. In 2015, I had the pleasure of taking one of Jason's Multicultural Counseling classes. This class awakened me to all of the societal and familial programming we experience and helped me take a step inward to look deeper into my beliefs and myself. It was a divine intervention and I am grateful.

Everything and everyone has been a blessing and miracle in my life. Thank you for the lessons and love.

I invite you to continue your work with Spirit in Volume 2 of this series.

I'll be waiting for you with love …

Made in the USA
Charleston, SC
18 January 2017